MW01615503

Windy City PULP STORIES #13

Celebrating the

100th Anniversary of Fu Manchu and his creator, Sax Rohmer

and the

90th Anniversary of the Science Fiction and Fantasy magazines

Compiled and edited by Tom Roberts

BLACK DOG BOOKS

2013
Normal, IL

"Fu Manchu: The First Hundred Years" by William Patrick Maynard © 2013 the author.

"The Fraudulent Fu Manchu" by Rick Lai © 2013 the author.

"J.C. Coll: A Retrospective Gallery" by Tom Roberts © 2013 the author.

"Margaret Brundage" by Robert Weinberg and R.A. Everts © 1988, 2013 the authors.

"From Pulp to the Silver Screen, 2013" by Ed Hulse © 2013 the author.

The publisher wishes to thank the following individuals for additional contributions made to this volume: Gene Christie, Doug Ellis, John Coker and Neil Mechum.

This edition, editing, arrangement and presentation © 2013 by Black Dog Books. All rights reserved. Except for brief passages for critical articles or reviews, no portion of this book may be reproduced in any form or by any mechanical, electronic or other means, now known or hereafter invented including photocopying, xerography, and recording, or in any information retrieval and storage system without the express written permission of the publisher.

ISBN 13 978-1-884449-41-3

Editing, book layout and design: Tom Roberts.
Proofreading: Doug Ellis, Gene Christie.

Cover art by Margaret Brundage.
Back cover art by Howard Browne.

Black Dog Books, 1115 Pine Meadows Ct., Normal, IL 61761-5432.
www.blackdogbooks.net / info@blackdogbooks.net

CONTENTS

Fu Manchu and Sax Rohmer

Fu Manchu: The First Hundred Years...........................William Patrick Maynard.......5
Sax Rohmer . . . Says Gangsters Doomed (1931 interview).............Gene Cohn.....26
Fu Manchu Photo Gallery..30
The Art of Making Villains (1924 Rohmer article)...42
The Fraudulent Fu Manchu...Rick Lai.....45

Weird Tales

Editors You Want To Know: Farnsworth Wright......................E. Hoffman Price.....53
Printing Company Occupies Washington Street Plant
    (Weird Tales printer in 1924) 56
Farnsworth Wright: Correspondence to Donald Wandrei, 1932...............................57
Weird Tales Club Card. 60
The Psycho-Mystic, Horror and Weird Story Field...............Joseph Lichtblau.....63
Market Requirements Pseudo-Scientific Magazines, 1936 69

Special Fiction Section

Ooze (reprinted from *Weird Tales,* Vol.1, No.1) ....Anthony Rud.....80

The Science Fiction Magazines

Novelty—The Essential of Science Fiction............................Charles D. Hornig.....98
The Science Fiction Field .... Leigh Brackett...104
E.E. "Doc" Smith Correspondence to Jack Darrow, 1931-38 ....Doug Ellis...118

Art Focus

J.C. Coll: A Retrospective Gallery...Tom Roberts.....18
Margaret Brundage .... Robert Weinberg / R.A. Everts.....71

Filmfest Focus

From Pulp to the Silver Screen, 2013 ....Ed Hulse...125

Index to Advertisers 133

NBC Radio photo promoting Rohmer's appearance on the first installment of the network's adaptation of his novel, *Yu'an Hee See Laughs*. Photo from the Gordon Lutz Collection.

Fu Manchu: The First Hundred Years

WILLIAM PATRICK MAYNARD

The first Fu Manchu novel, *The Mystery of Dr. Fu-Manchu,* was published 100 years ago in 1913. US publication (as *The Insidious Dr. Fu-Manchu*) followed within four months of the British edition. The book's success on both sides of the Atlantic spawned a successful series of titles that spanned nearly fifty years. The character quickly made the transition to film, newspaper strip, radio drama, comic books, and (eventually) television. Dr. Fu Manchu was quickly established as the archetypal criminal mastermind of pulp fiction. Despite this fact, the character's origins were not in the pulps, but in the slicks.

The Devil Doctor's creator, Arthur Henry Ward, was born in England in 1883. His father hoped his son would make his way through life as a respectable businessman, but young Arthur was determined to make his name as a writer. He discovered immortality with the invention of two unlikely monikers that conjured an air of exotic intrigue when they debuted in print a century ago. The first was his chosen pen name, *Sax Rohmer* and the second was the name of his most famous character, *Dr. Fu Manchu.*

A few decades on, Rohmer would allege a real Chinese criminal called Mr. King served as the basis for the character. Mr. King was actually a more realistic version of Fu Manchu that the author created for his 1914 novel, *The Yellow Claw.* Rohmer later attempted to revive the character for his 1932 novel, *Yu'an Hee See Laughs,* but it proved unpopular. Shortly thereafter, Rohmer began claiming that Mr. King was real. Sadly, like many of Rohmer's claims (including his and Bram Stoker's membership in The Hermetic Order of The Golden Dawn and the Rosicrucians), this was more a question of fiction than fact.

Over the years, the insidious villain's name lost its hyphen and became synonymous with a moustache that his creator never intended the character to wear (although illustrators and actors thought otherwise; much like Sherlock Holmes' ever-present deerstalker). Rohmer concocted an amalgamation of Professor Moriarty (from Sir Arthur Conan Doyle's Sherlock Holmes stories) and Dr. Nikola (from Guy Boothby's then-popular series of novels about a similar criminal mastermind). The result was the personification of the Yellow Peril that had gripped the West since the Boxer Uprising at the turn of the century.

Standing in sharp contrast with the racist stereotype conjured by the name, the literary Fu Manchu is a well-spoken, highly-educated, and surprisingly honorable scientist who serves a secret society opposed to British colonial interference in the East. Using a variety of scientific devices (some of his own devising), a menagerie of poisonous insects, and an army of exotic assassins, he sets out to

The first appearance of Fu Manchu was
in the October 1912 issue of *The Story-Teller*—the same month
in which Tarzan debuted in *The All Story.*

eradicate those who stand in his path if they refuse to heed his warnings.

Most intriguing in our post-9/11 world, the Devil Doctor chooses to fight his battles not in China, but on British soil with acts of terror. He is opposed in his efforts by stalwart British colonialist Nayland Smith and a dizzying array of companions who chronicle Smith and Fu Manchu's secret war. As Rohmer continued the series over five decades, his characters aged in real time. While the early stories avoided all mention of the First World War, later novels made world events and thinly-disguised versions of real life figures part of the rich tapestry that Rohmer wove.

Dr. Fu Manchu made his first appearance in October 1912 in the short story, "The Zayat Kiss," a thrilling tale patterned after Sir Arthur Conan Doyle's "The Speckled Band" complete with the Holmesian duo of Burmese Police Commissioner Nayland Smith and his loyal friend and assistant, Dr. Petrie. Readers of Britain's *The Story-Teller* were delighted with the results and the story became the first of a collection its author titled simply, *Fu-Manchu*. The unflappable duo of Smith and Petrie repeatedly strive to save those who know too much from assassination. The colorful intended victims range from the Reverend J. D. Eltham who gained notoriety as "Parson Dan" during the Boxer Uprising to the bombastic Egyptologist and adventurer, Sir Lionel Barton (Rohmer's humorous take on Sir Richard Burton). The beautiful and mysterious Karamaneh, an agent of Fu Manchu, becomes the love of Dr. Petrie's life and repeatedly saves our heroes when they find themselves in her master's clutches. Ironically, Karamaneh is unwilling to leave Fu Manchu's service as the life of her sickly brother depends upon her continued cooperation.

"Kâramanéh," the sixth of the Fu Manchu stories, furthered the love interest between the Devil Doctor's beautiful slave and Petrie.
Collier's, April 26, 1913

The first series of stories were collected in book form in 1913. The fix-up proved a success and readers clamored for more. For a time, Sax Rohmer was quite happy to deliver. A second series of stories entitled *Fu-Manchu and Company* first appeared in the US in the pages of *Collier's* from November 1914 through December 1915. The collection was published in book form as *The Devil Doctor* in 1916. US publication as *The Return of Dr. Fu-Manchu* quickly followed the British edition. Nayland Smith and Dr. Petrie were back for Round Two against Dr. Fu-Manchu and his minions with return appearances for Karamaneh, Aziz, and Reverend Eltham.

There was little question at this point that a third series of stories would follow. By the time the second fix-up made it into bookshops, the new series, *The Si-Fan Mysteries* was appearing in *Collier's* (April 1916 to June 1917). Upon the series' conclusion, it was published in book form (retaining its magazine title for the first time) while Rohmer's US publisher opted for *The Hand of Fu Manchu*. It was the American publisher who first discarded the Devil Doctor's hyphenated name for the title, but not the text. Thereafter, all future stories would follow suit and the character's name was printed as "Fu Manchu" from that point forward. This time around Nayland Smith and Dr. Petrie liberate Karamaneh once and for all, discover the Si-Fan is the name of the secret society Fu Manchu serves, and succeed in saving Sir Lionel Barton from assassination yet again.

All three of these series conclude with a question mark hanging over Fu Manchu's final fate leaving the door open for a further series. Despite their success, Rohmer had grown tired of the formula and wished to concentrate on other work. Interestingly, he returned to his detecting duo of Smith and Petrie (albeit anonymously) for the short story, "The Blue Monkey" which appeared (in Britain only) in his 1920 collection of short fiction, *The Haunting of Low Fennell.*

Fu Manchu's successful transition to the silver screen in the 1920s (in two silent movie serials starring Harry Agar Lyons for Stoll and an

Sax Rohmer, whose Fu-Manchu stories thrilled you, starts a new series—"The Si-Fan Mysteries"— describing the battle of wits between a diabolically clever Oriental organization and a famous English detective. The first, a tale complete in itself, appears in this week's issue of

A prominently placed advertisement, running on page five of the *New York Times,* April 4, 1916

early talkie feature starring Warner Oland for Paramount) made it inevitable that requests for a literary sequel would follow. Rohmer acquiesced in 1928 when he signed an agreement with *Collier's* to bring the Devil Doctor back. His first attempt was abandoned and reworked as a non-series entry. Readers would have to wait until March 1930 when the magazine began serializing Rohmer's new novel, *Fu Manchu's Daughter* just a few weeks ahead of Warner Oland's second appearance in the role for a brief segment of the film *Paramount on Parade* and the studio's near-simultaneous release of a second Warner Oland Fu Manchu feature film loosely based on Rohmer's second book. A radio dramatization of each installment of *Fu Manchu's Daughter* was broadcast as part of *The Collier Hour.* The title of the new novel would be altered slightly to *Daughter of Fu Manchu* for its publication in book form in the UK and the US the following year. The book was followed shortly by Paramount's third and final Warner Oland feature, *Daughter of the Dragon* whose title sought to capitalize on Rohmer's new bestseller despite the fact that the studio did not own the rights to the book in question.

As noted above, Rohmer allowed his characters to age in the decade since their last appearance. Nayland Smith was now graying and had been knighted and was presently serving as Assistant Commissioner of Scotland Yard. Readers also learn his Christian name is Denis. Dr. Petrie, long since settled down to wedded bliss with his beloved Karamaneh, returns but his role as Smith's sidekick and chronicler has been taken by a new character, an engaging half-caste known as Shan Greville who was employed by Sir Lionel Barton. Fu Manchu's imposing height and startling green eyes had always pointed to his own mixed heritage. Rohmer had noted that Karamaneh was an exotic mixture of Egyptian and European blood. Fu Manchu's daughter, Fah lo Suee (who first appeared anonymously as a teenage temptress in the third book) is now a full-grown femme fatale and we learn that her mother was a Russian beauty. The xenopho-

Dustjacket art for *The Hand of Fu Manchu,* 1920.

bia that fed into Yellow Peril fiction was slowly being undermined by Rohmer's fascination with foreign cultures. He had moved from having his heroes fall under the spell of these exotic characters and lands to now having a half-caste for a hero and not having any of his other characters comment on the fact in the process. This was quite a radical concept for a series that is often dismissed as racist out of ignorance or willful political correctness.

Interestingly, Rohmer next chose to rework "The Blue Monkey" as "The Mark of the Monkey" when it was published in *Brittania & Eve* in April 1931 (just as Leo O'Mealia's *Fu Manchu* newspaper strip made its debut). This time around, Rohmer identified Smith and Petrie under their own names. A third Nayland Smith story without Fu Manchu, "The Turkish Yataghan" appeared in *Collier's* in January 1932. Rohmer utilized Shan Greville as Smith's Watson for this tale. Both of these stories subsequently appeared in the British edition of Rohmer's short story collection, *Tales of East and West* in 1932 although only the latter story appeared in the US edition of the title in 1933.

The success of *Daughter of Fu Manchu* guaranteed a sequel. *Collier's* serialized *The Mask of Fu Manchu* in May and June of 1932. Doubleday, Rohmer's US publisher, rushed the title into bookstores to capitalize on MGM's big budget film

The Mask of Fu Manchu
Doubleday, Doran and Co. 1932

adaptation starring Boris Karloff and Myrna Loy released in November of that year. British readers would have to wait a year until the UK edition appeared in shops.

By that time, a CBS radio series entitled *Fu Manchu* had already proven a success with 31 half-hour episodes airing between September 1932 and April 1933. By the time the radio adaptations concluded, Leo O'Mealia was likewise completing his newspaper strip adaptations. The Devil Doctor had mastered magazines, books, film, newspaper, and radio in the twenty years since his introduction. There would be no rest for the character any time soon.

Collier's began serializing a new novel, *Fu Manchu's Bride* in May 1933. Doubleday kept the title intact for the US edition while the UK market offered a slight variant with *The Bride of Fu Manchu*. Rohmer left Shan Greville in peace having wed Sir Lionel Barton's niece. Nayland Smith's latest sidekick and chronicler was a dashing young English botanist called Dr. Alan Sterling. Dr. Petrie still figured in the proceedings as the unfortunate young woman who has been raised in captivity to bear Fu Manchu an heir turns out to be his daughter. Not only would Fleurette learn the identity of her parents over the course of the novel, she would also find love with Alan Sterling in this interesting reworking of the original formula. The plot of this novel concerning biological warfare was almost certainly an influence on Ian Fleming's *On Her Majesty's Secret Service*. Fleming was a devoted fan of the series and patterned *Dr. No* on the Devil Doctor. Before all was said and done, the creator of James Bond would have a decisive role to play in the series' future.

A direct sequel, *The Trail of Fu Manchu* appeared in *Collier's* beginning in April 1934. Hardback editions in the UK and US appeared in due course. This time out, Rohmer abandoned the first-person narrative. The results are less satisfying although readers were happy to see Fleurette win her freedom and settle down to become Mrs. Alan Sterling. Fu Manchu's plot this time out involving an alchemical furnace fed with the bodies of human beings is undoubtedly the character at his most heinous. Rohmer also appeared to have killed off Fah lo Suee with her sadistic father seemingly executing his daughter for betraying him to Nayland Smith. Part of the success of the formula lay in the fact that the ever obsessive Smith sublimates all sexual desire to concentrate on his goal the same way the Devil Doctor does to concentrate on his various schemes. Rohmer eventually comments upon this peculiar fact more explicitly as the line between the characters begins to blur. Interestingly, Rohmer's publisher requested an additional chapter to give the novel a more sentimental conclusion. Rohmer acquiesced, but was displeased with the results. Consequently, some later editions omit this chapter.

Collier's began serializing a new Fu Manchu novel, *The Invisible President,* in February 1936. The title was changed to *President Fu Manchu* for the UK and US hardback editions later that year. Third person narrative was again employed. The plot (which revolves around a corrupt US presidential election featuring characters based on Huey Long and Fr. Charles Coughlin) appears to have influenced Richard Condon's *The Manchurian Candidate.* Rohmer himself had a hand in adapting his series for a British radio series, *Dr. Fu Manchu,* which was broadcast over the course of 52 fifteen minute episodes from December 1936 to November 1937. By 1938, *Detective Comics* was featuring newly-colored versions of the Leo O'Mealia newspaper strip as a recurring feature as the Devil Doctor now made the transition to comic books.

President Fu Manchu
Crime Club, 1936

Collier's brought the Devil Doctor to the brink of the Second World War in April 1939 when they began serializing Rohmer's new novel, *The Drums of Fu Manchu,* just weeks ahead of the debut of a US radio series, *The Shadow of Fu Manchu,* which dramatized the entire series (including *The Drums of Fu Manchu*) over the course of 156 fifteen-minute episodes broadcast from May 1939 to June 1940. Rohmer successfully returned to a first person narrative format with the introduction of Fleet Street journalist Bart Kerrigan as Nayland Smith's latest Watson. The plot concerned thinly disguised versions of Hitler and Mussolini targeted for assassination by the Si-Fan. Some may find it interesting that Rohmer placed his own published views on preventing a Second World War into the mouth of Fu Manchu rather than Nayland Smith. The author also very nearly remade the original Fu Manchu storyline with Kerrigan falling in love with Fu Manchu's exotic Eurasian agent, Ardatha. Hardback editions of the book made it into UK and US shops just as war in Europe was beginning to appear inevitable.

Republic Pictures filmed a 15-chapter movie serial loosely based on *The Drums of Fu Manchu* that debuted in March 1940. *Liberty*, perhaps the most prestigious of the slicks to carry Rohmer's fiction, serialized a direct sequel,

Fu Manchu and the Panama Canal, starting in November 1940. Bart Kerrigan was back as the narrator-hero and succeeded in winning Ardatha away from the Si-Fan and thereby bowing out of both Nayland Smith and Fu Manchu's world. Hitler and Mussolini now appeared under their real names. For the first time, Rohmer had to backtrack as world events had overtaken his fiction and he was now forced to declare portions of his last book to be fictionalized accounts demanded by the Foreign Office. This clever excuse would soon take on greater significance. Hardcover editions of the book were subsequently published in the UK and the US the following year under the title, *The Island of Fu Manchu,* containing very minor differences in the text between each edition.

Rohmer claimed that the Second World War hurt the series, alleging that the Foreign Office prevented his publishers and other potential partners from utilizing the character for fear of offending their Chinese allies. There is no proof of this and the similarity to the Foreign Office fictional excuse in his last Fu Manchu novel makes the claim rather suspect. The truth of the matter is that during the Second World War, Republic Pictures edited their *Drums of Fu Manchu* serial down to feature film length and re-released it to theatres in November 1943 and NBC broadcast a new 30-minute radio adaptation of the first Fu Manchu novel in August 1944. Rohmer's own efforts during these years were largely spent in trying and failing to produce a Fu Manchu Broadway play. Rohmer had written several other stage plays during his long career, but true theatrical success continued to elude him. There is no evidence to suggest that an eleventh Fu Manchu novel was attempted until the late 1940s. Likewise, rumors of a planned second serial by Republic Pictures being blocked by the US government are unsubstantiated. Republic's subsequent release of the feature-length edit of their Fu Manchu serial would seem to disprove the veracity of this claim. Another Fu Manchu movie did go before the cameras in Mexico where the Spanish-language *El Otro Fu-Man-Chu* was filmed in 1946.

When Rohmer did revive the series, it was as a hasty rewrite of his unproduced stage play. *Collier's* began serializing Rohmer's first Cold War Fu Manchu thriller, *The Shadow of Fu Manchu,* in May 1948. Doubleday rushed the book into US stores that same year where it became Rohmer's final New York Times bestseller and the last original Fu Manchu title to have a hardback edition in the US. British readers would be forced to wait until the following year for hardcover publication of the title.

A direct sequel, barely numbering 80 pages, was serialized in *The Toronto Star Weekly* in January and February 1952 under the bizarre title of "Green Devil Mask." The length and limited market suggest the fact that the series' popularity was rapidly fading. Rohmer recycled portions of the text for his third Sumuru novel, *Virgin in Flames,* published later that same year. (Sumuru was a character Rohmer first created for BBC radio during the Second World War as a female variation on Fu Manchu. A series of five novels featuring the character were published in the 1950s. Interestingly, Rohmer chose to rework characters and situations from his 1929 novel, *The Emperor of America,* for the Sumuru series.

The Destiny of Fu Manchu
by William Patrick Maynard

A chance encounter with a beautiful woman at an Egyptian wedding leads archaeologist assistant Michael Knox on a whirlwind journey to Cairo.

A chain of events quickly unfold that embroils Knox with obsessive British agent, Sir Denis Nayland Smith, and his pursuit of the master criminal, Dr. Fu Manchu. Slowly, the young man pieces together the threat posed to the world as Fu Manchu and his seductive, but sadistic daughter, Koreani, dismantle the dreaded secret society, Si-Fan.

But before Knox can act on the intelligence in his possession and stop Fu Manchu, he must survive a series of diabolical assassination attempts.

As madness sweeps the globe, Knox struggles to keep apace. Sweeping action, from Greece to Egypt to Africa to Europe, carries the battle at a breathtaking pace as the fate of the world in the balance in *The Destiny of Fu Manchu . . .*

Available in hardcover, trade paperback, Kindle, Nook, ePub, or PDF from

BLACK COAT PRESS
http://www.blackcoatpress.com/
info@blackcoatpress.com

The Emperor of America had started life as the abandoned fourth Fu Manchu novel Rohmer attempted in the late 1920s before rewriting it as an original work. Whether he realized it or not, Rohmer had come full circle forty years after introducing the Devil Doctor.) Rohmer scholar, Dr. Robert E. Briney, rescued "Green Devil Mask" from obscurity, re-titling the novella, "The Wrath of Fu Manchu" for publication in the UK in 1973 as the title story in a posthumous bargain-priced hardcover collection of Rohmer's short fiction. A paperback edition of the collection was published in the US three years later.

NBC also produced a 30-minute unsold pilot for a Fu Manchu television series starring John Carradine in 1952. Rohmer scripted the pilot utilizing an unproduced teleplay he had written for the BBC in 1949 based on "The Zayat Kiss." A syndicated series of 13 half-hour episodes was eventually produced by Republic Pictures in 1956 under the title, *The Adventures of Dr. Fu Manchu.* Rohmer was involved in a contentious lawsuit over the rights to the series that stretched on to the final weeks of his life and led to the premature cancellation of Republic's

Sax Rohmer and his wife, Elizabeth, bound for New York aboard the ocean liner *Majestic,* 1932. Photo from the Gordon Lutz Collection.

planned 39 week series. Happily, the television revival proved beneficial to Rohmer in opening the market for Fu Manchu paperback originals in the US. Rohmer penned *Re-Enter: Fu Manchu* for Fawcett Books in July 1957. A hardcover edition was printed in the UK under the variant title, *Re-Enter: Dr. Fu Manchu.*

A Canadian Sunday supplement, *This Week* published three Fu Manchu short stories commencing with "The Eyes of Fu Manchu" in October 1957. "The Night Fu Manchu Learned Fear" followed in March 1958. The story was re-titled "The Word of Fu Manchu" when it was reprinted in *Edgar Wallace Mystery Magazine* in February 1966. This was the title Dr. Briney retained for its inclusion in the posthumous collection, *The Wrath of Fu Manchu.* The last Fu Manchu short story was published as "Fu Manchu and the Frightened Redhead" by *This Week* in February 1959. Rohmer's preferred title was "The Secret of the Flying Saucer." *Edgar Wallace Mystery Magazine* re-titled the tale "The Mind of Fu Manchu" when it was reprinted for its March 1966 issue. Once again, Dr. Briney retained this later title for the posthumous collection of short fiction he edited in the 1970s.

Rohmer's final novel *Emperor Fu Manchu* was published in June 1959 just weeks before his death. The title was again written as a paperback original for Fawcett Books in the US, but received a hardcover edition in the UK. Happily, it was Rohmer's best work for the series since *The Island of Fu Manchu*, the novel it most closely resembles. Rohmer fell ill with the Asiatic flu epidemic that spread through the US at the time. Despite his ailing health, he could not resist leaving the door open for a promised sequel that he would never live to write. Rohmer's widow wrote to Ian Fleming shortly after her husband's death requesting the creator of James Bond consider continuing the series. Mr. Fleming kindly declined telling her that the series' time had passed. Mrs. Rohmer heeded his advice although she later sold all movie and television rights to the character in the 1960s (resulting in the five Christopher Lee Fu Manchu films of the decade as well as a pair of Shirley Eaton Sumuru movies). She also licensed Marvel Comics to incorporate the Fu Manchu characters in their martial arts titles, *Master of Kung-Fu* and *The Deadly Hands of Kung-Fu* which introduced another generation to the property in the 1970s. A regrettable Peter Sellers spoof, *The Fiendish Plot of Dr. Fu Manchu,* proved a box office disappointment when it was released just weeks after the actor's death in 1980.

Following Mrs. Rohmer's passing, her husband's long-time assistant and co-author (with Mrs. Rohmer) of the only book-length biography of her husband [1972's *Master of Villainy*], was authorized by the Sax Rohmer Literary Estate to continue the series. His first effort, *Ten Years beyond Baker Street* (1984) was set 70 years in the past and saw Sherlock Holmes coming out of retirement to aid Dr. Petrie after Nayland Smith is abducted by the Si-Fan. Cay Van Ash did an excellent job of capturing the style of both vintage Rohmer and late period Conan Doyle. The novel also afforded Dr. Petrie the welcome opportunity to play Watson to Holmes.

Van Ash's second effort, *The Fires of Fu Manchu* (1987) was again set 70 years in the past and saw Colonel Nayland Smith and Dr. Petrie tussling with the Si-Fan during the First World War. The novel was also noteworthy for an appearance by a teenaged Fah lo Suee and an explanation for how Nayland Smith comes to be knighted. Both of Van Ash's titles are well-written and build upon the existing continuity. Cay Van Ash passed away in 1994. At the time of his death, he had been working on a third novel, tentatively titled *The Seal of Fu Manchu* for several years. The manuscript is believed lost.

There have been several further attempts to re-launch Fu Manchu on the silver screen since the 1970s, but thus far only a Spanish-language soft-core pornographic film [1986's *Esclavas del Crimen*], a further Spanish-language comedy short [1990's *La Hija de Fu-Manchu*] and Nicholas Cage's parody trailer in 2007's *Grindhouse* have actually made it before the cameras. Happily, the Sax Rohmer Literary Estate granted me the honor of allowing me to author, to date, two more Fu Manchu continuation novels, both published by pulp-specialty publisher, Black Coat Press. 2009's *The Terror of Fu Manchu,* was set on the eve of the First World War while its 2012 sequel, *The Destiny of Fu Manchu,* was set on the eve of the Second World War.

That brings us to the character's centennial as Titan Books nears the mid-way point of their ambitious re-printing of the original series. A century after his first appearance, Rohmer's prediction that the character would survive long after his creator had passed on has proved accurate or, as Christopher Lee would intone at the conclusion of his 1960s Fu Manchu films, "The world shall hear from me again."

Ad in the *Newark Advocate,* July 29, 1916.

The Sax Rohmer Library
from Black Dog Books

Series Editor: Gene Christie

THE VOICE OF KALI

Collected for the first time comes this volumes of strange happenings and weird mysteries ... Paul Harley, the private investigator of Chancery Lane, and star of Rohmer's novels *Bat Wing* and *Fire Tongue,* embarks to uncover the truth behind seven unexplainable and odd murderous events.

With an introduction by
William Patrick Maynard
(The Destiny of Fu Manchu)

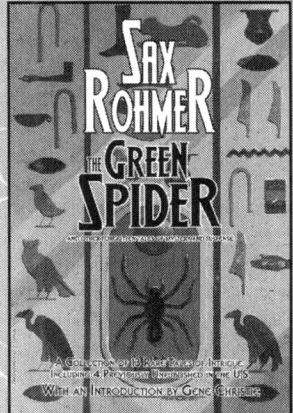

THE LEOPARD COUCH

204 pp / $19.95
13 more tales by the incomparable Rohmer await the reader, *including 4 stories never published in the US!*

With an introduction by
F. Paul Wilson
(Lifetime Achievement Award recipient from the Horror Writers of America)

THE GREEN SPIDER

13 rare mysteries, *including 4 tales previously unpublished in the US!*

"Fine, creepy stuff!"
—Mystery Scene

Follow us!
Twitter.com/blackdogbooks1
Facebook.com/blackdogbooks1

www.blackdogbooks.net I info@blackdogbooks.net

17

J.C. Coll:
A Retrospective Gallery

TOM ROBERTS

Beginning with "The Zayat Kiss," Sax Rohmer's first fiction for *Collier's,* the job of illustrating these dramatic stories was assigned to J.C. Coll (1881-1921). A virtuoso with the pen, Coll grasped the work of Rohmer firmly with both hands and pulled forth one beautiful drawing after another from its prose.

As the readership of Rohmer grew, so did the exposure of Coll. When Rohmer's stories were syndicated for newspapers from their *Collier's* appearances, often the original images by Coll accompanied them.

J.C. Coll's sudden death from appendicitis at age 41, it was a tremendous loss to the art world.

In addition to his assignments for the work of Rohmer, Coll also illustrated contemporary, adventure and fantasy fiction for a variety of well-known authors including Arthur Conan Doyle, Talbot Mundy, Abraham Merritt, Edgar Wallace, Victor Rousseau, Charles Dickens and others in such magazines as *Everybody's, Century* and *Redbook,* as well as books and newspaper sections.

"Kâramanéh," *Collier's*, April 26, 1913

"The Zayat Kiss," *Collier's*, February 15, 1913,
the first Fu Manchu story.

An early rendition of the Devil Doctor.
One-half of a two-page spread from
"The Clue of the Pigtail," *Collier's*, March 1, 1913,
the second Fu Manchu story.

Left: "The Clue of the Pigtail," *Collier's*, March 1, 1913.

Coll's quintessential face-off between Fu Manchu and Nayland Smith.
From "Kâramanéh," *Collier's*, April 26, 1913.

From "The Silver Buddha," *Collier's*, May 15, 1915.

From "Zarmi of the Joy Shop," *Collier's*, May 13, 1916.

From "Queen of Hearts," *Collier's*, November 25, 1916.

Sax Rohmer, noted author of mystery stories, is pictured above with his wife. He is in this country to look the American market over for new sinister characters to put in his books.

Sax Rohmer, Creator of Villainous Characters, Says Gangsters Doomed

GENE COHN

Fu Manchu, most sinister of contemporary villains, has been "taken for a ride."

After eight years of devilish, macabre exploits, this slant-eyed prince of evil has been "put on the spot" by our own American gangsters, racketeers and gunmen.

All this is reluctantly admitted by Sax Rohmer, who introduced the Oriental archfiend to millions of persons over the land. Rohmer is now engaged in prowling through the gang hangouts of New York and Chicago, guided by "undercover" men and friendly racketeers. He's looking the American market over for new sinister characters, and he concedes that they have been "chiseling in" on Fu Manchu's racket. In the face of so much, real life blood-and-thunder, a good old-fashioned hair-raiser finds real competition, he admits a bit sadly.

A SLAVE RUNNER

So Rohmer has turned temporarily to a piratical sort of cuss he calls Yu'an Hee See, who runs slave girls and opium across the Red Sea. This is a bit closer to the rum-running sort of things familiar to American audiences. Some day Fu Manchu may be resurrected but he doesn't know when. However, Fu's creator is quick to rush to the defense of his villain and to condemn the gangsters and racketeers.

"At least Fu Manchu lived because I made him a mysterious and romantic figure," says Rohmer. "And it's my opinion that your gangster problem will be solved—if it is—by the cheap and sordid methods they themselves employ. The public seems to have become accustomed to them over here, though it's beyond me to figure out how they ever got so well organized and strongly entrenched.

"But whatever romance may have attached to these figures in the beginning is dying. They have become too petty and crooked.

"Yes, Fu Manchu may have been an arch-villain and all that. But remember, he never did anything for gain. His intrigues were largely political. He was an individual, a personality—not a product of gang and mass criminality.

"I have made quite a study of villains, in and out of fiction. The public will accept a villain quite as quickly as it will a hero—in fact history seems to have quite a preference for personalities who were slightly or totally wicked.

"Outside of a group of good church people, who can name more than three or four saints? But every youngster knows all about Cleopatra. Francois Villion remains one of the most romantic of the poetic figures, though he was a drunkard, a thief and an all-round rascal.

Reprinted from *The Niagara Falls Gazette,* Thursday, March 12, 1931

"It's this romantic element that your gangsters are forgetting about. They're too greedy, too money mad, too practical to become heroic villains. I have a theory that your public will not stand for them a great deal longer, for after all the Americans are a romance loving people."

It was Mrs. Rohmer, an attractively blonde English girl, who at this point suggested that villains were particularly attractive to women readers.

"But there's one thing that is slightly annoying," she commented. "And that's the fact that my husband always uses my newest clothes on his strangest villainesses. If I come home with a new coat or a new hat, it's almost certain that this raiment will appear on the most impossible women of his fiction. It's his little way of getting even for having to foot the bills, I suppose.

"After all, I do sometimes wish he'd dress his women a bit differently and stop using my clothes on them."

WAR ON GANGS

Fu Manchu, Rohmer explains, came into being slightly more than eighteen years ago at a time when the author was one of the Fleet Street aggregation. The character was patterned after an old Chinese met by Rohmer while writing police news for a London newspaper.

"It was this fellow's appearance, rather than anything he had done that gave me the idea," says Rohmer. "The fellow was merely a fence, where thieves took their stolen goods. But he had a face like the faces seen in a nightmare—wrinkled, warped and evil.

"It had not occurred to me at the time that a character of such villainous nature could become so popular—but I had not gone so deeply into the study of villainy as I since have. Humans have always been fascinated by horror, and probably will be for some generations.

"But when this horror gets too close to the home and fireside, something will be done about it. And so, I have an idea that the incredible crime conditions in your country have just about reached their peak. I think, too, that the average good citizen has remained inactive because the gangsters staged their fights among their own kind and seldom came out of this boundary—but racketeering has begun to hit the average man and woman in one way or another, so I am told, and you can begin to see the reaction.

"On the morning I arrived in New York, the first newspaper I picked up was filled with news of scandals growing out of crooked politics. A few years ago, I am informed, no one would have cared much. At the moment your gangs seem well organized and tremendously powerful, but it needs only a bit of internal dissension to blow this all up—as your gang wars have proved. They are all afraid of each other, if not of the law. They will kill themselves with greed. I think."

Do you like a thrilling mystery---

and a good love story?

Then Read

THE GREEN EYES OF BAST

Beginning Monday, May 22

THE

Philadelphia Bulletin

Will print this thrilling tale of Egyptian mystery and cunning,
by Sax Rohmer,
the author of the Fu Manchu Stories

The Goddess of Bast
(The Cat-Woman)

Out of the darkness of Egypt she came. The Egypt of the Cat Goddess Bast: the Egypt of the great Pyramid builders: the Egypt of thousands of years ago.

She is not Egyptian, yet like the Cat Goddess "in her treacherous moments she played with her victim as with a mouse before finishing him off with her claws."

There is not a dull paragraph in "The Green Eyes of Bast." You will be fascinated by the story of this mysterious creature whose identity is never guessed until the very end.

Who was the Cat-Woman? What was She?

This remarkable story of mystery, keen detective work--and love

THE GREEN EYES OF BAST

Begins Monday, May 22 in

The Philadelphia Bulletin

Full page newspaper advertisement from 1922 for Rohmer's latest novel serialization.

Fu Manchu On Film:
A Photo Gallery

Editor's note: Many actors and actresses have been associated with the Fu Manchu canon since it was first introduced to the film world in 1923 with the release of a series of silent shorts including *Aaron's Rod, The Call of Siva, The Clue of the Pigtail* and others. H. Agar Lyons appeared as Dr. Fu Manchu opposite Fred Paul as Nayland Smith in 23 silent outings between 1923 and 1924.

What follows is a selection of stills from some of the better known presentations of Fu Manchu with their famous leading actors at their most dramatic and diabolical.

Warner Oland enjoys the solitude of his thoughts. *The Mysterious Dr. Fu Manchu* (1929).

Left: Warner Oland resorts to the use of the blade in *The Mysterious Dr. Fu Manchu.*

Warner Oland in *The Mysterious Dr. Fu Manchu*. Oland was also
cast as the lead in 1930's *The Return of Dr. Fu Manchu*.

Warner Oland and O.P Heggie as Nayland Smith in *The Mysterious Dr. Fu Manchu.*

Anna May Wong as Princess Ling Moy in Paramount's *Daughter of the Dragon* (1931), based on Rohmer's novel, *The Daughter of Fu Manchu.*

The seductive Anna May Wong in *Daughter of the Dragon*.

Anna May Wong in *Daughter of the Dragon*.

Alyn Warren, Warner Oland and Anna May Wong in *Daughter of the Dragon.*

Christopher Lee takes the lead in *The Face of Fu Manchu* (1965).

Boris Karloff in *The Mask of Fu Manchu* (1932).

Boris Karloff in *The Mask of Fu Manchu*.

One reviewer wrote: "Karloff is the center of a formidable combination of intrigue, strange crimes and fiendish punishments. There is, for instance, the mysterious laboratory where Fu Manchu hurls his man-made lightning and his sinister 'death ray.'"

Myrna Loy, Charles Starrett and Boris Karloff in *The Mask of Fu Manchu.*

Charles Starrett is
still a long way off
from his signature role of
The Durango Kid while
portraying Terrence
Granville in 1932's *The
Mask of Fu Manchu.*

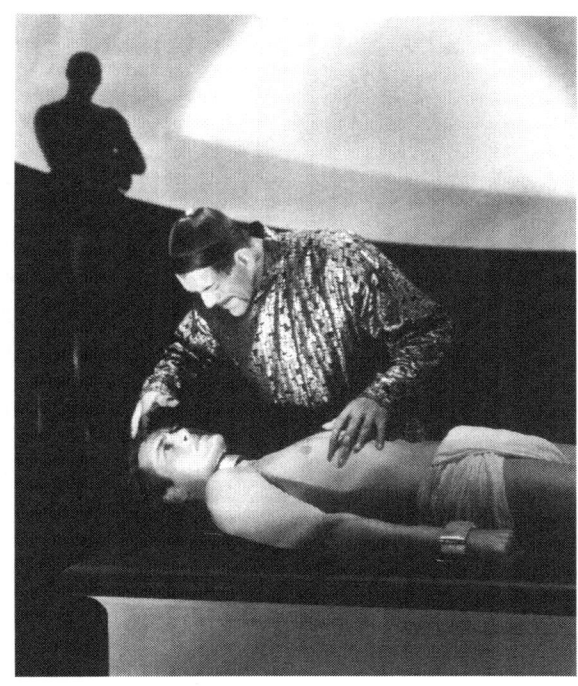

Myrna Loy as Fa Loh See in *The Mask of Fu Manchu*.

The Art of Making Villains

SAX ROHMER, FAMOUS "THRILLER" WRITER, TELLS HOW HE RAN AWAY FROM SUCCESS.

Sax Rohmer, who has created more numerous and fascinating villains than any-one since Gilbert and Sullivan admits that this art of thrill making was not entirely a natural gift. It was developed by a series of experiments with various other pro-fessions, each of which gave him some special bit of knowledge or ingenious idea for the alluring black magic of his stories. From "Dr. Fu Manchu" to "Brood of the Witch Queen," his new book just released by Doubleday, Page & Co., Rohmer has flashed against richly exotic backgrounds such diabolical ingenious and irresist-ible villains as one trusts this world has ever seen.

Sax Rohmer's own dizzy career has been a series of valiant attacks of fortune and hasty retreats when he met her face to face. He has always intended to be an author and although he assures a biographer that he wrote nothing worthy of men-tion before the age of 4, his first serious work, "The Man In the White Hat," was written sometime during his early school days. The boy had fallen under the spell of Mark Twain and this story was the outcome. It was rejected by every periodical published in Great Britain.

At the age of 19, young Sax had one wall of his den papered with a de-sign made up of editorial regrets. By this time, there were ten or a dozen short stories that had traveled separately over the entire United Kingdom. Forced to the conclusion that editors were not reading his stories, the youthful author hit upon the scheme of affecting writing paper of unusual color and envelopes of extra-ordinary size. Nothing happened. Finally two stories were accepted within twenty-four hours of each other. One editor asked Rohmer to eat and suggested that he do a series of stories dealing with the same character. The shock was nearly fatal. The boy immediately left England and wrote no more for five or six years. He studied in several art schools with the intention of becoming a black and white artist, although he met with nothing but discouragement. Being young, failure stimulated immensely. He worked day and night and bombarded the illustrated press with drawings. Then one day "Judy" accepted a drawing and asked him to call. From that day to this, he has done no more drawings.

Abandoning art, Rohmer converted a studio into a rehearsal theatre and with three partners prepared a one-act play for the variety stage. They finally secured a "trial week," but the playlet "got the hook," and thus closed this dramatic epi-sode.

The next plunge was into musical composition, but the music publishers were not impressed. With ditties and light concert numbers, however, Rohmer had fair

Reprinted from the *Oakland Tribune,* April 20, 1924, p.101

success. A friend introduced him to a famous concert artist, for whom he immediately wrote a character song that the artist resolutely declined to sing. Spurned to renewed efforts, he wrote others and finally the artist tried one with success. Things went swimmingly. One or two musical compositions were published. Then came the end. The artist offered him a contract and a music publisher in London requested him to join his staff.

Immediately Rohmer got into touch with a tramp steamer skipper and was arranging a voyage to South America when a long-missing friend, a medical student, turned up with a scheme for putting a new kind of moth ball on the market. After feverish periods of chemical activity the two young promoters were forced to admit that the mothballs failed to attract. In an idle moment, Rohmer rewrote an old story that elicited from a publishing house a proposition to continue the series definitely. It was a crucial moment. A steamer carrying general cargo was leaving the Thames for Spanish ports on the following morning. Rohmer resisted the temptation and stayed in London to complete the first series. Since then other pursuits no matter how alluring have failed to entice him away from his most fascinating of occupations, the art of villain making.

IT LOOKS MYSTERIOUS—Sax Rohmer, well-known English author of thrillers, directs a penetrating gaze at New York's sky line as he arrives on the S. S. Berengaria. He is here to make an extensive study of American crime control and possibly to write a new mystery story with an American background. Mrs. Rohmer arrived with him.

Danville Breeze
(Danville, NY)
May 31, 1935

Original artwork for sale

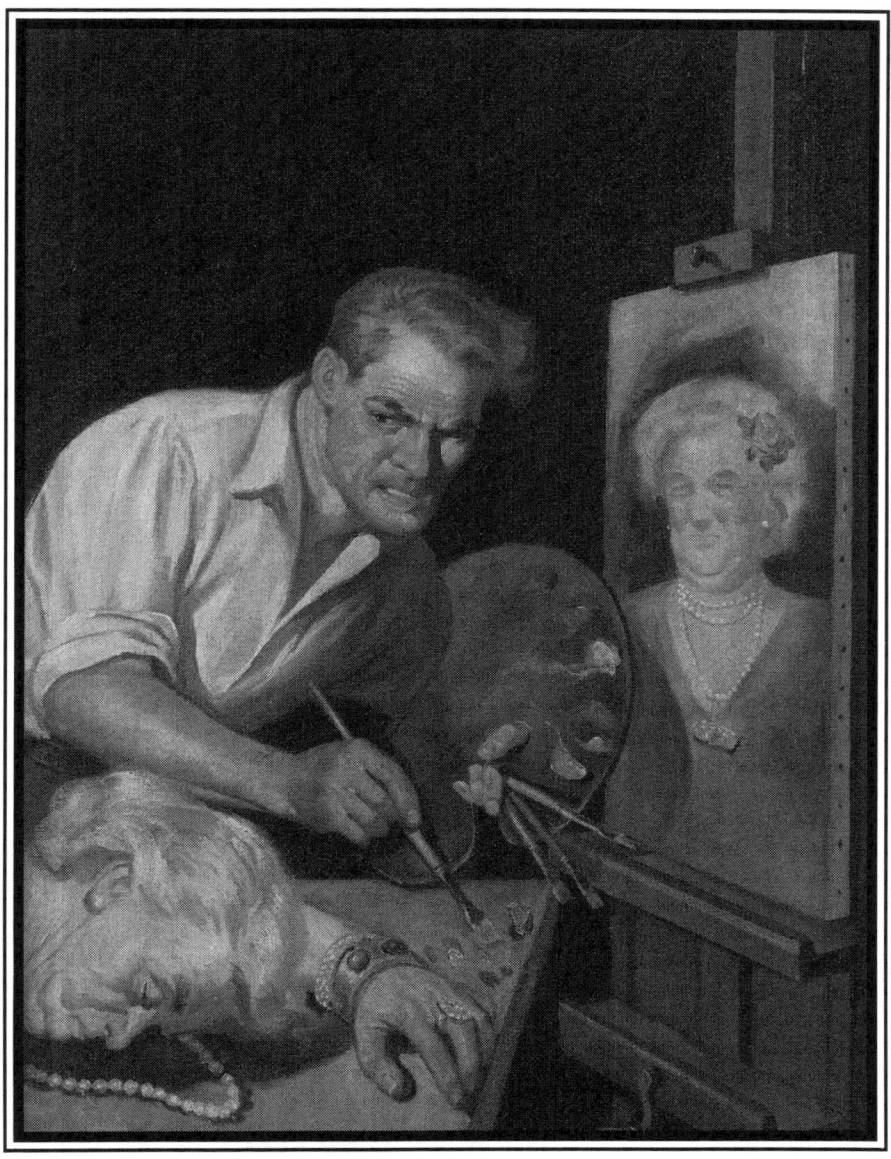

RAPHAEL DESOTO
Cover art for *Dime Detective Magazine,* November 1944 / Oil on canvas

TARABA ILLUSTRATION ART
(307) 333-2517
www.tarabaillustrationart.com / fred@tarabaillustrationart.com

44

The Fraudulent Fu Manchu

RICK LAI

In 1975, I picked up a paperback edition of Philip José Farmer's *Doc Savage: His Apocalyptic Life*. I looked at the genealogical chart linking various fictional characters in the front of the book. Being an ardent fan of Sax Rohmer, I was intrigued by an entry for Fu Manchu. Who was this Hanoi Shan whose name was in parentheses next to Fu Manchu? Flipping through the book, I discovered that Hanoi Shan was a master criminal whose career had been documented by an author of non-fiction, H. Ashton-Wolfe (1881–1959). According to Farmer, Hanoi Shan was the real-life inspiration for Rohmer's Fu Manchu.

Hanoi Shan was supposedly an actual governor of a province in French Indochina. After being hurled by an elephant into a tree, Hanoi Shan's back was severely damaged. He was now a hunchback. Maddened by his ordeal, he became a crime boss in Paris. Feared as "the Spider," his arsenal included cataleptic gas, a female impersonator, poisonous centipedes and a hypnotic device that transformed men into criminals.

Harry Ashton-Wolfe is not generally considered a pulp author. However, several stories from his book, *The Invisible Web* (1928), were serialized in *Detective Fiction Weekly* starting with the issue dated December 1, 1928. Writing as H. Ashton-Wolfe, the vast majority of his stories appeared in *American Weekly*, a Sunday magazine published by the Hearst newspaper empire. In this tales, Ashton-Wolfe featured crimes as bizarre as those depicted by Sax Rohmer, Walter Gibson or Seabury Quinn. Nevertheless, these stories were presented as non-fiction. Ashton-Wolfe was one of the greatest liars of all time.

Trying to clarify the facts of Ashton-Wolfe's life is difficult because he's our primary source of information. Apparently, he was the son of a Scottish doctor who served with the Eighth United States Calvary stationed in New Mexico.

Detective Fiction Weekly, December 1, 1928

Although born in London, he spent his childhood in Arizona and Colorado. In the early 20th century, he supposedly served with the Surete, the French police, in Monte Carlo, Paris and Lyons. He was an assistant to two great forensic scientists, Alphonse Bertillon (1853-1914) and Edmond Locard (1877-1966). Some editions of *The Invisible Web* identified Locard as co-author, and that French investigator confirmed his association with Ashton-Wolfe publicly. During World War I, Ashton-Wolfe was allegedly a British spy operating in Belgium.

One aspect of Ashton-Wolfe's life can definitely be confirmed. In 1923, he was serving as the French translator for the British courts. Two extraordinary murder trials happened in that year. In both cases, the defendant spoke French and no English. Marguerite Fahmy shot her husband, an Egyptian prince, in a London hotel. Jean Pierre Vaquier poisoned a British innkeeper. Ashton-Wolfe acted as interpreter for both of the accused. Madame Fahmy was exonerated (on grounds of self-defense) while Monsieur Vaquier was sent to the gallows.

Ashton-Wolfe wrote of these cases in a book called *The Underworld* (1926). He also included "true" accounts of his career as a Surete operative and a British spy. Seven books followed. These mainly concerned his exploits with the Surete, but two books dealt with historical crimes.

As his writings progressed, the crimes supposedly investigated by Ashton-Wolfe became more and more outrageous. Some of these criminals encountered by Ashton-Wolfe really existed. These actual felons include the Bonnot-Garnier gang of bank robbers, Mata Hari the World War I spy, the murderous Dr. Pierre Bougrat, and Red Lopez the Utah bandit. However, other lawbreakers are clearly made up. Several are mad scientists who act like characters from horror movies. For example, there is "The Mystery of the Floating Bodies" from *Strange Crimes* (1932). The malefactor in that story beheaded men and kept their brains alive (like Peter Cushing in *Frankenstein Must be Destroyed*). Other evildoers are clearly inspired by Fu Manchu and the Oriental villains popularized by Sax Rohmer.

Best known of the fraudulent criminals manufactured by Ashton-Wolfe is Hanoi Shan, a Chinese hunchback who supposedly lorded over the French underworld in the early 1900's. The first two tales about Hanoi Shan, "The Suicide Room: Hanoi Shan" and "The Scented Death: Hanoi Shan" were collected in *Warped in the Making* (1927). Two more stories, "Kiki: A Tale of Hanoi Shan, the Spider" and "Chang Foo Lee" appeared in the British edition of *The Thrill of Evil* (1928). The 1930 American edition of the same book replaces "Chang Foo Lee," with "The Devil's Telephone," a story that doesn't feature Hanoi Shan. At least three additional exploits of Hanoi Shan were never collected in book form, but appeared in the pages of *American Weekly*. Unfortunately these stories have no titles because *American Weekly* frequently printed Ashton-Wolfe's accounts as chapters of a book.

The first Hanoi Shan story, "The Suicide Room," may be a plagiarism of a famous horror story by Hanns Heinz Ewers (1871-1943), "The Spider." This tale was highly praised by H.P. Lovecraft in his famous essay, "Supernatural Horror in Literature." "The Spider" was written in 1907. A new translation by Joe E. Bandel

The Terror of Fu Manchu
by William Patrick Maynard

The death of a seemingly respectable missionary draws Denis Nayland Smith and his devoted companion, Dr. Petrie, back into the web of the diabolical Dr. Fu Manchu.

Our heroes are led on a harrowing journey where they cross paths with the Si-Fan, a rival Theosophist society and the famous French detective, Gaston Max.

The clash of Eastern and Western cultures sharply contrasts with the age-old battle between the forces of Good and Evil, as Nayland Smith and Petrie grapple with the fragile truths that rule their world.

Moving rapidly between London and Paris in 1913, this action-packed thriller is the first new Fu Manchu novel in over twenty years and reintroduces the Devil Doctor and his deep-seeded plots of world domination to an entire new generation of readers!

Authorized by the Sax Rohmer estate.

Available in hardcover, trade paperback, Kindle, Nook, ePub, or PDF from

BLACK COAT PRESS
http://www.blackcoatpress.com/
info@blackcoatpress.com

can be found in *Hanns Heinz Ewers: Volume 1* (Order of Anarchistic Knights, 2009).

"The Spider" related a series of deaths in a hotel located on the Rue Alfred Stevens in Paris. The story opened with three successive tenants having apparently committed suicide in the same hotel room. All of the dead men were founding hanging from a hook on a window crossbar. Since the window is low, none of the corpses were found hanging in the air. Each of the man seemingly strangled themselves by bending their knees on the floor.

A fourth man, a medical student named Richard Bracquemont, rented the room. He soon discovered himself haunted by a sort of changeling that could take the form of both a woman and a spider. Ashton-Wolfe had Hanoi Shan, a master criminal called the Spider, behind virtually identical murders in a hotel in the Rue Lhomond.

Ashton-Wolfe claimed that there was an account of these crimes in the *"Chronique de Tribunaux,"* 1907-08. Since I don't have access to these documents, I can't verify the criminologist's claims. However, the similarities between the works by Ewers and Ashton-Wolfe are too much to be a coincidence. There are

H. Ashton-Wolfe

multiple possible explanations for the parallels. First, Ashton-Wolfe actually told the truth about this 1906 crime. Ewers then based his 1907 story on a real event. Second, Ashton-Wolfe invented his account of Hanoi Shan by re-working the elements of Ewers's story. There is a third possibility. Ewers could have based his fiction on an actual crime that Ashton-Wolfe falsely attributed to a non-existent Asian mastermind. All the evidence points to Ashton-Wolfe plundering the works of Ewers.

There exists another convergence between the works of Hanns Heinz Ewers and H. Ashton Wolfe. In 1908, Ewers wrote "The Death of Baron Jesus Maria von Friedel " Like "The Spider," this story can be found in the recent *Hanns Heinz Ewers: Volume I.* Like Norman Bates from Robert Bloch's *Psycho* (1959), Jesus Maria von Friedel was a schizophrenic man whose other personality was feminine. In his alter ego. Friedel dressed up as a woman. Eventually, Friedel committed suicide with a gun. However, the author argued that this was really murder. One of the two competing personalities had slain the other.

In *Warped in the Making,* Ashton-Wolfe recorded "The Murder of Don Ramon Valdes Y Cazal." Don Ramon had the same personality disorder as Baron von Friedel. Don Ramon was found poisoned. The French police initially suspected murder. When the truth was learned about Don Ramon's double life, it was concluded that the death was technically suicide. The female personality had left a poisoned decanter for the male counterpart. Ashton-Wolfe professed that the details of the case were documented in *"Gazette des Tribunaux,"* Paris edition, July to August 1909.

In a rather wild subplot, it was revealed that Don Ramon's in his female identity had once gone to Haiti in order to become a voodoo priestess. There was a rather vivid description of the sacrifice of a child in a voodoo ceremony. This scene was very similar to an episode form Ewers's

"Blood," a novelette that was translated into English in 1930, but which seems to have been published in German before World War I.

Ashton-Wolfe became friendly with Sir Arthur Conan Doyle, the noted mystery writer. Ashton-Wolfe dedicated *Outlaws of Modern Days* (1927) to Doyle. At least one of Ashton-Wolfe's renditions of a factual crime influenced a story by Doyle, *Warped in the Making: Crimes of Love and Hate* includes the story of Mario Allivi, a swindler who attempted to sell a phony death ray to the Italian navy. This event became the basis for Doyle's Professor Challenger story, "The Disintegration Machine." Challenger even alluded to Allivi in the course of the story: "We have not forgotten a recent case where an Italian, who proposed to explode mines from a distance, proved upon investigation to be an arrant impostor."

Seabury Quinn, the author of the Jules de Grandin stories in *Weird Tales*, clearly read Ashton-Wolfe. Dr. Sun Ah Poy, the only recurring adversary to fight de Grandin, is a virtual copy of Hanoi Shan. Sun appeared in "The Lost Lady" (*Weird Tales*, January 1931) and "Satan's Stepson" (*Weird Tales*, September 1931). The villain of Quinn's "The Brain Thief" (*Weird Tales*, May 1930) may have been inspired by Chundah Lal, a Hindu hypnotist who robbed people of their memories. Chundah Lal appeared in two stories from *The Thrill of Evil,* "The 'Happy Death'" and "The Passing of the Euthanasia," as well as a third untitled story in *American Weekly*.

In order to support his wild claims, Ashton-Wolfe reproduced photographs that allegedly depicted the people and objects from his stories. Occasionally Ashton-Wolfe was careless with his photographic evidence. In the pages of *American Weekly* , the photograph of the same tattooed man was used for three distinct criminals in three different stories. "Leaves of Lethargy" (*American Weekly*, October 27, 1940) had a voodoo criminal equipping zombies with a circular pistol. A photograph of this weapon was produced. Supposedly the zombie master invented this weapon in the 1900's. Actually, it's a French firearm, the Protector, patented in 1882 by Jacques E. Turbiaux.

Ashton-Wolfe's literary career seems to have peaked in 1932. He sold the film rights to his "true" Surete accounts to David O. Selznick of RKO pictures. Selznick was hoping to make a series of B movies featuring Frank Morgan, the actor best known for playing the title character in *The Wizard of Oz,* as Ashton-Wolfe. According to the Turner Classic Movie (TCM) website, the RKO legal department discovered that Ashton-Wolfe's accounts were full of blatant falsehoods. Subsequently, only one film, *Secrets of the French Police* (1932), was released. The name of Frank Morgan's character was changed from Harry Ashton-Wolfe to Francois St. Cyr. The screenplay was based on Ashton-Wolfe's "The Mystery of the Orly Highway" and two

untitled storied from *American Weekly,* as well as Samuel Ornitz's *Lost Empress,* an unpublished novel about Princess Anatasia of Russia.

According to the TCM website, Ashton-Wolfe was under investigation by the British and French authorities for fraud in 1932. If this is true, he was never arrested. He continued to write stories for *American Weekly* until 1940. However, the authorities of another country did apprehend him. Ashton-Wolfe made the mistake of residing in San Remo, Italy. In June 1940, Benito Mussolini declared war on the British Empire. Ashton-Wolfe was interred as an enemy alien.

When the Allies invaded Italy in 1943, they located Ashton-Wolfe. In January 1944, he told an horrific account of his incarceration by the Fascists to the *London Times.* He does not seem to have written any new stories after World War II, although some of his earlier tales were published in South Africa during the 1950's. He died at the age of 78 in Sussex during July 1959.

Hanoi Shan had largely been forgotten until the false theory that this "real-life" mastermind was the basis for Sax Rohmer's Fu Manchu was circulated. The idea was first proposed in John Harwood's "Speculations on the Origin of Dr. Fu Manchu" (*The Rohmer Review #2,* January 1969) before *Doc Savage: His Apocalyptic Life* (1973) widely publicized the premise that Hanoi Shan's crimes influenced Fu Manchu. In actuality, the popularity of Rohmer's novels prompted Ashton-Wolfe to create Hanoi Shan.

All seven known stories about Hanoi Shan will be reprinted in 2013 by Battered Silicon Dispatch Box as *The Crimes of Hanoi Shan.*

Journey To Worlds Unknown
with Black Dog Books

BEYOND THE POLE
PHILIP M. FISHER

Discover the bizarre happenings in these eleven unforgettable tales. Encounter a strange race of Sargasso Sea-like weed men; ship out on a vessel that sails into a weird magnetic fog; battle against a madman that can put the world in total darkness; journey by dirigible to the North Pole to investigate strange happenings and more! With an introduction by weird fiction authority and anthologist Stefan Dziemianowicz.

L'ATLANTIDE
PIERRE BENOIT
Travel into to the heart of the Sahara and discover lost Atlantis ... and its eternal queen! With a foreword by David Hatcher Childress (History Channel, *Ancient Aliens*).

THE AIR TRUST
GEO. ALLAN ENGLAND
A vicious capitalist plots to take control of the world's air supply and force the population to pay for the air they breath.

Follow us!
Twitter.com/blackdogbooks1
Facebook.com/blackdogbooks1

BLACK DOG BOOKS
1115 Pine Meadows Ct.
Normal, IL 61761-5432

www.blackdogbooks.net I Info@blackdogbooks.net

Farnsworth Wright (1888–1940), editor of *Weird Tales* from 1925 to 1938.

He was a perfectly wonderful man. He was a very tall man, six feet three
or four inches, with a boyish face. Even at this period he was very far gone
with his disease—Parkinson's Disease. . . . He had this stumbling gait and an
extremely bad palsy. . . . He had a wonderful sense of humor.

—Margaret Brundage on Farnsworth Wright

Editors You Want to Know:
Farnsworth Wright, Editor of *Weird Tales*

E. HOFFMANN PRICE

"First of all," declared Farnsworth Wright as he shooed from the editorial rooms of *Weird Tales* a handful of loitering ghouls, vampires, and ghosts, "I insist upon there being a story. Authors only too often confuse story material or story setting with the story itself. The transplanting of a human brain into the skull of an ape would be an interesting surgical experiment; but a tale based on such a feat is acceptable only when the results of the transplanting are dramatic and striking.

"The pseudo-scientific story which is now so much in demand must do more than outline a fanciful invention or process entirely beyond the reach of present scientific achievement. The author must develop a plot which derives its major interest not from the pseudo-scientific principle itself but from an ingenious solution based on a startling application of that principle.

"Tales which carry the hero to distant planets come to my desk by the score. But in most cases the characters, after having been projected into interstellar space, experience commonplace adventures they could much more readily have found on earth.

"Ghost stories of the right kind are welcomed; but we invariably reject those which describe nothing but the terror inspired by the mere appearance of a ghost. These are old fashioned. When Sir Walter Scott wrote 'The Tapestried Chamber,' he gave a splendid example of a ghost story in which nothing happened except that someone was frightened almost to death because he saw a ghost. If a ghost story is to make the grade, it must possess motivation and characterization rather than be a rubber-stamped catalogue of wails, apparitions, and clammy hands.

"Again, a weird tale must be convincing. Because we use stories that are frankly impossible, authors are surprised when their work is rejected as not being plausible. The point is that while a concededly impossible hypothesis can be accepted by the reader, the story is satisfying only if the sequence of events based on the impossible is logical and consistent. We can accept a ghost, a vampire, or an evil spirit only when unusual and dramatic action rather than mere presence is the substance of the story. The supernatural as such is by no means adequate; and since we deal with the impossible, it is all the more necessary that they should be convincing; that they should *seem* real.

"We have printed tales of vampires vividly and humanly characterized instead

Reprinted from *Author & Journalist,* October 1931.

of being obscured by a timeworn litany of garlic and holly sprigs; and we have presented stories whose point was not the personal appearance of Satan, but rather his unusual reaction to a startling and dramatic situation. There were truly great weird tales, which, through their scarcity, are always in demand.

"Finally, our ideal is the presentation of a story having literary value. Very often we accept a tale which though not emphasizing the weird, the supernatural, or the pseudo-scientific, merits approval on account of its rich color, exquisite workmanship, bizarre philosophy, and strong plot."

Now let us turn from quotation to a sketch of the man himself:

Farnsworth Wright tumbled into the magazine business before he was out of grammar school in San Francisco, where he not only wrote and edited a publication called *The Laurel*, but set the type and printed it on a hand press, being editor, author, printer's devil, compositor, and pressman.

During his last two semesters in college he was managing editor of the University of Washington *Daily*. After graduation he was a reporter for the Chicago *Tribune,* and the Chicago *Herald-Examiner,* and later, music critic of the last named. He then left the newspaper game to edit a magazine called *Health,* whose brief career was soon ended by the untimely death of the publisher.

While occupied as reporter and editor, Wright was selling stories to *Munsey's* and other magazines. When *Weird Tales* made its appearance, he sold material which appeared in its initial issues; and later, he read manuscripts for both *Weird Tales* and *Detective Tales*. Shortly thereafter, when the Popular Fiction Publishing Company took over *Weird Tales,* he became publisher. He is now launching a new magazine, *Oriental Stories*.

Thus, baldly sketched, we have his history. But those who have heard its ups and downs from Wright himself when coffee and cigars follow dinner at Le Petit Gourmet, not far from the editorial rooms on Michigan Boulevard, can best understand why "Pious Plato" goes to such pains to encourage promising beginners: for in each beginner Wright sees himself again fighting his way from ham and eggs. Personal rejections, accompanied by bits of constructive criticism, have made of a good many beginners prime members of Wright's circle of chronic contributors. Wright, the editor, is first and last the friend of the author.

Wright served during the World War as an interpreter in the A.E.F. His repertoire, in addition to French, includes Spanish, German, Italian, and a touch of Russian: all of which is an outcropping of his taste for the foreign and colorful. Kouskous, pilau, and East Indian curry are his favorite dishes; Latakia and Darjeeling suit his tastes, respectively, in tobacco and tea; and when he's thirsty . . . well, he mixes an unusually fragrant drink with Bacardi, limes, and pineapple juice as the basic principles.

Finally, his favorite weakness must be mentioned: limericks!

"Farnsworth, recite the one about the young man from Bombay."

"If only I had a time machine!"

NO NEED FOR A TIME MACHINE. BUY PULP REPLICAS FROM ADVENTURE HOUSE, NOW WITH MORE THAN 450 ISSUES IN STOCK...PRICES RANGE FROM $3 TO $14.95. THREE NEW TITLES A MONTH.

Adventure House - 914 Laredo Rd - Silver Spring, MD 20901

Industrial Indianapolis In Review

Printing Company Occupies Washington Street Plant

The new plant of the Cornelius Printing Company, 2407-59 East Washington Street, is another step in the growth of the company, since business in Indianapolis was started nearly twenty-five years ago. Publication of the *American Legion Weekly,* will begin in the new plant with the issue of Dec. 19th, and 700,000 to 800,000 copies will be printed each week.

The plant, which has been under construction more than four months, is a one-story building, containing approximately 30,000 square feet of floor space, part of which will be devoted to the business offices of the legion publication. The feature of the plant is that all of the departments are centralized on one floor, making possible a higher degree of efficiency in printing and publishing work. The building is constructed of tile and glass on four sides. It is more than twice the size of the former plant of the Cornelius Company on North Capitol Avenue.

New equipment has been added to take care of the larger volume of work to be done by the company. In addition to the printing of the Legion magazine, the publication of other magazines will be continued, including the *United Mine Workers Journal,* of which 800,000 copies are printed bimonthly, and *Weird Tales,* a 192-page monthly magazine with a circulation of 100,000 copies. The *Legion Weekly* will be printed in its present form with the exception of the cover. A special two-color cover will be printed beginning with the Dec. 19th issue.

Officers of the *Legion Weekly* came to Indianapolis from New York to take charge of the printing of the publication, and will maintain headquarters at the Cornelius plant.

The Cornelius Company has occupied its Capitol Avenue plant for about fourteen years. George M. Cornelius is president and treasurer of the company, George H. Cornelius, secretary, and A.M. Cornelius, vice president.

Reprinted from *The Indianapolis Star,* Monday, December 8, 1924, p.3

Farnsworth Wright: Correspondence to Donald Wandrei (1932)

Editor's note: One of the many tasks of any editor is staying in touch with his authors. This letter from Farnsworth Wright to Donald Wandrei is interesting in its discussion of author Nictzin Dyahlis, a writer on whom verifiable biographical information has eluded researchers, sparking speculation that Nictzin Dyahlis was a pseudonym, yet Wright claims this to be the writer's actual name.

The story "Moss Island" that Wright comments to Wandrei's inquiry about is presumably "Moss Island" by Carl Jacobi, which was published in the recently appearing Winter 1932 issue of *Amazing Stories Quarterly*. Jacobi, a fellow Twin Cities resident and later friend of the Wandrei's, submitted "Moss Island" to *The Quest,* his high school literary magazine upon a request from a teacher seeking the work of alumni for inclusion and "Moss Island" ran in the May 1930 issue. Jacobi, reworking the story, sold it two years later to the paying market of *Amazing Stories Quarterly.*

Within a year of this letter, Jacobi would join Wandrei as a contributor to *Weird Tales.*

No serial by Wandrei ever appeared in *Weird Tales.*

Donald Wandrei
1152 Portland Avenue
St. Paul, Minn.

840 N. Michigan Ave.   Chicago, Ill.

EDITORIAL ROOMS

March 23, 1932

Donald Wandrei
1152 Portland Avenue
St. Paul, Minn.

Dear Wandrei:

          I think this chap Low, who claims
that he wrote WHEN THE GREEN STAR WANED,
under the pen name of Nictzin Dyalhis, is all
wet. Nictzin Dyalhis is a real person, and
that is his real name. He is a man well
on in years, and is a personal friend of
Arthur Sullivant Hoffman, former editor of
ADVENTURE. His father was an English sea
captain named Dyalhis, which is one of the old-
est English names. His mother was a Guatemalan
with some Toltec Indian blood in her. Nictzin
is a Toltec Indian name. If any further check-
up on Low is needed, I might say that the checks
were all made out to Dyalhis in his own name,
and that none of them went anywhere near St. Paul.

          I am surprised about your reading MOSS
ISLAND in both WEIRD TALES and AMAZING STORIES
QUARTERLY. I cannot think which story you mean
by MOSS ISLAND, for we have had no story of that
name in WEIRD TALES.

A MAGAZINE of the BIZARRE and UNUSUAL

840 N. Michigan Ave.   Chicago, Ill.

EDITORIAL ROOMS

#2

       Four months ago we were in the market for serial stories; but now we are stocked up on serials to run nearly to the end of 1933. I have a five part serial story by Victor Rousseau starting in our July issue; this will be followed by a six part story by Kline; and I have serials on hand by Hugh Davidson and A. W. Bernal to follow these. I would of course be glad to have a serial from you, but do not like to ask you to wait for payment; and yet the magazine business is so poor at present that we cannot pay until publication.

       I hope you will be passing through Chicago soon again. If you do, please don't fail to drop in.

       Best regards.

             Sincerely yours,

             Farnsworth Wright,
             Editor

FW:MM.

The Weird Tales Club Card

Editor's note: This rare bit of ephemera was issued by *Weird Tales* in 1940s, after the magazine was bought and its offices relocated from Chicago to New York. Like other premiums issued by pulps, this was an attempt to expand the magazine's customer base though interaction and interest between fellow readers.

How many club cards were issued is unknown. Few have survived, making it a highly sought after premium on the collectables market.

FANTASY ILLUSTRATED

PULPS FOR SALE!

Thousands of pulps in stock. We love servicing your want lists.

■

Contact DAVE SMITH

(425)745-0229 • (425)750-4513

rocketbat@msn.com

■

40 years experience in
the paper collectibles field.

Prompt professional service.

Specializing in Pulp Magazines,
Vintage Comic Books, BLBs,
Pin-up material and Houdini.

■

Pulps wanted!

High prices paid. All genres wanted.
One piece or a lifetime collection. No
collection is too large or small.

P.O. Box 13443
Mill Creek, WA 98082

FANTASY ILLUSTRATED

visit www.fantasyillustrated.net

Ian Fleming called him the model for **James Bond**.

Lester Dent said he influenced **Doc Savage**.

The *Original* Adventure Hero Comes to Audio
In An Exciting New 5-Hour Full-Cast Audio Drama

BULLDOG DRUMMOND
The Audio Adventure

Pulp Radio presents a new audio drama from the original Bulldog Drummond novel starring pop music icon and radio host

Ian Whitcomb

plus a cast of Hollywood's finest voice artists.

In extra-dimensional stereo, with full sound effects and period music score.

WINNER!
2013 AVA
Platinum Award
for Audio

Available NOW in a deluxe 6-CD set or immediate MP3 download at
PulpRadio.net

Human Interest Stuff

"Rodney Schroeter and William Messner-Loebs have revived that time-honored but half-forgotten pulp subgenre, the sentimental dog story. You will never forget Tatters!"—Will Murray

Like a good story? Good art? Dogs?

This comic book adaptation is available for $4.00 from Rodney Schroeter, or visit:
www.tinyurl. com/his-apt

HUMAN INTEREST STUFF from the story by Albert Payson Terhune
Adapted by Rodney Schroeter and William Messner-Loebs
32 pages plus covers, magazine size (8.25 x 10.5 inches)
Color covers, black and white interiors | Visit www. tinyurl. com/his-apt

The Psycho-Mystic, Horror and Weird Story Field

JOSEPH LICHTBLAU

With the advent of the new Clayton magazine, *Strange Stories,* into the field of psycho-mystic, horror and weird stories, writers will now find a market of such interesting possibilities for future financial profit, that I feel this article should be of the most timely interest to you who have really fertile imaginations. In the past, *Weird Tales* offered a rather limited field for psycho-mystic, occult, weird, ghost, supernatural, vampire, voodoo, obi, werewolf, reincarnation, mystic, psychic stories, since other magazines did not use them. *Argosy,* however, would occasionally consider stories of these types. Do not confuse *Amazing Stories* and *Amazing Stories Quarterly* with magazines of the *Weird Tales* type, for the first two publish only stories based on science, and, unless you knew science well enough to build imaginary images around it skillfully enough to "get by," you are very much out of luck.

As for *Miracle, Science and Fantasy Stories,* which used stories somewhat similar to *Amazing Stories* and *Amazing Stories Quarterly,* the former is now overstocked anyway, and wants no further material.

There are now the following markets wide-open for the type of stories referred to in the title of this article; each one has certain definite requirements which I will try to outline as specifically as possible:

(1) *Strange Stories,* 80 Lafayette St., New York City, Harry Bates, editor. (2) *Weird Tales,* 840 N. Michigan Ave., Chicago, Ill., Farnsworth Wright, editor. (3) *Mind Magic,* 1008 W. York St., Philadelphia, Pa., G. M. Bay, editor. (4) *Ghost Stories,* 570 7th Ave., New York City, Dan Wheeler, editor. (5) *Argosy,* 280 Broadway, New York City, Don W. Moore, editor.

A recent form letter from Harry Bates, editor of *Strange Stories,* states the following:

> The Clayton Group is now buying stories for a new magazine to be devoted exclusively to material of the weird type. In it we welcome stories of the occult, weird, ghost, supernatural, vampire, voodoo, obi, werewolf, reincarnation, mystic, psychic kinds. . . . Shorts for this should not exceed 8000 words, and novelettes should run between 25,000 and 30,000 words. No serials. . . . . These stories may contain woman interest and be laid in any part of the world. It is extremely

Reprinted from *Writer's Digest,* August 1931.

important that in these are stressed the elements of mystery and terror. We want the reader to shudder and be mystified and fascinated and wholly enthralled until the story is over. There may be a sizable touch of horror. They should be neither highbrow nor cheap and thrilling trash, but well constructed stories of good quality that will appeal to a wide range of readers. . . . Two cents a word and up on acceptance.

Any magazine that pays 2c a word on acceptance is worthy of study. Since I haven't seen *Strange Stories* on the stands yet, I urge you to get, as fast as possible, *Mind Magic* and *Weird Tales,* and to read both so thoroughly that you will soak your mind on the individual "slant" of their contents. For, if you have *Mind Magic* and *Weird Tales* as a guide, you will have a darned good working idea of what *Strange Stories* will be like.

Also, if you want still another fine guide, by all means get *Ghost Stories,* too; for in this magazine you will find ghost and super natural yarns exclusively, while *Mind Magic* and *Weird Tales* use practically every type of tale mentioned in the Clayton form letter. Too, if you buy *Argosy* and come across a fantastic yarn there, study that story with all your powers of concentration, for such a fantastic yarn may be just the inspiration you need to hit *Strange Stories.*

Permit me to give you a brief synopsis of a story I sold to *Mind Magic,* which appeared in the August 1931 issue.

The title of my story is "As a Man Thinks—" My hero was a business executive who let his prosperous business go to the dogs because his pessimistic sister urged economy in every direction. He cut down his staff of employees, discharged most of his household servants, smoked cheaper cigars and wore cheaper clothes, and instead of his former luxurious car, he used a small, cheap one. Bankers, quick to note the changes and listen to the rumors of the gossips, refused my business executive hero credit; and he was about to slide into bankruptcy when a most odd, amazing experience saved him.

On the banks of a small

Ghost Stories, June 1931.

stream, he saw an old, queer-looking chap of ancient garb fishing. The old gent got the hero to confide in him, and told him that the reason he was about to fail was because he had given people the impression of sudden poverty. Impressed by the advice of the old gentleman, the hero returned to town in a taxi, with an impressive gardenia in his lapel and a fine cigar in his mouth, looking as if he had suddenly fallen heir to unexpected wealth.

As a result, his credit was renewed; bankers loaned him all he wanted; and in a year's time, he was once more a business success. When he re-visited the stream, the old fisherman no longer was there; and the hero then discovered he

Mind Magic, June 1931.

was but an apparition out of a long-ago abandoned cemetery! Thus he learned the great lesson: "As you think, so you are! As you will, so shall you attain! For the mind and the spirit conquer everything.

Now, as you can readily see, while this gem packs a sound moral and theme, it is, of course, nothing but a ghost story, and, of course, far-fetched. Yet it so impressed Mr. Bay, editor of the magazine, that he bought it. And why? Because in *Mind Magic,* good must always conquer evil in some stories; in other yarns, great good must be achieved through right thinking; if the occult and the mystic are featured, they must always help the protagonists in some concrete way; black magic must always be defeated by "white" magic-white magic, of course, representing the best and noblest in humanity. So you can easily see that *Mind Magic* is primarily a magazine of inspiration; and while the stories there may be as far-fetched and fantastic as possible, they must always leave the reader with a warm glow in his heart and never depress him too much.

To give you another concrete example of the type of fiction in this magazine: A widower buys a nude statuette of a woman who resembles his dead wife. In life, she had been so modest and virtuous that she even refused him his marital rights! He gloats over the statuette; manhandles it sadistically; feels he is getting a giant revenge on his dead wife because that nude statuette is so defenseless in his salacious hands. In the end, it falls down on his head and kills him! And, once again, good triumphs over evil, though, of course, the ending is a mighty convenient one for the author with which to bring out his moral lesson.

In *Weird Tales,* however, evil can "put it all over" good, and your stories will never offend the editor! So long as your yarns horrify the reader to a satisfying extent, fascinate, mystify him and make him shudder, you can go as far as you like, it seems. Of all the shuddery, creepy things I ever read, a recent story in *Weird Tales,* David H. Keller's "Seeds of Death," is a most significant example of the sort of yarn this magazine features.

It leads up to a climax wherein it is revealed that the woman fiend of the tale got her victims to swallow certain seeds found on the grounds of her isolated castle in Spain and, boy! what happened to those poor gents afterwards is enough to make your hair acquire a permanent wave! Those seeds sprouted inside the vitals of the unfortunates, and tree limbs grew out of their bodies while they lived, until they died most horribly!

Weird Tales, August 1931.

In another yarn in *Weird Tales,* a chap drank a certain poison concocted by a witch doctor in the African wilds and the poor guy shrank down, slowly and horribly, to the size of a new-born babe before he found a merciful death! And a most magnificent example of a fantastic story is Otis Adelbert Kline's novel, beginning in the July issue of *Weird Tales,* "Tam, Son of the Tiger." The hero is two years old when he is abducted by a tigress and reared by her in company with her own tiger cub! Attaining manhood, he meets a weird serpent woman, saves her life from a tiger who seems to have no regard whatever for the fact that Tam is practically a blood brother, and as the first installment ends, Tam is fighting off a bunch of four-armed giants from an underground world, and has just been knocked out!

I have briefly outlined types of stories found in *Mind Magic* and *Weird Tales,* to give you a fairly definite idea of the sort of tales you must create if you wish to hit

Strange Stories. Tales of sorcery and magical rites, yarns about werewolves, vampires, "dead-alive" horribles, so forth and so on, offer the writer with clever ideas and good imagination a field for exploitation that was never more profitable than today, when *Strange Stories* offers a new and additional market. With *Mind Magic* recently started and *Strange Stories* hard on its heels, there is a definite trend towards stories of these types now which is likely to continue until the public loses interest in them; so that, for the next year or so at least, you have a splendid opportunity to branch out from your "regular" stories very profitably.

For *Mind Magic,* confine your shorts to 1500 words at most, and you will have the proper length for Mr. Bay. He is overstocked on

Strange Tales, September 1931.

serials. He doesn't demand fine writing; the stories in his "book" are told very simply and humanly. He uses brief stories of true experiences with ghosts and the supernatural told in the first person in anecdote form; he also dotes on any fact article up to 1000 words that inspires the reader, such as articles on the super-mind, the magic of the book of psalms, mastery of yourself, information about astrology, etc. These articles will stand an even better chance if they contain good plot germs for fiction; I got my plot idea for "As a Man Thinks—" from a brief fact article in the first issue. A thorough study of the magazine is the best guide to it; 1c per word, on publication.

Weird Tales, however, demands a much better style; some of the yarns are written so impressively and in such a "high-brow" manner, that one wonders how talented authors could afford to contribute for 1c per word on publication—which is the rate for acceptable stories with this periodical. Lengths—shorts, up to 10,000—novelettes, to 15,000, serials up to 40,000.

Ghost Stories uses only the sort of yarns indicated by its title; no definite length requirements, apparently, and either first or third person. Always wide open for material; 1c up, acceptance.

In my opinion, it is well worth studying all the magazines suggested in the beginning of this article, simply on the chance that you may hit *Strange Stories* as a result. Steeping yourself in the atmosphere and "feel" of these magazines, if you have any creative imagination whatever, is bound to inspire you wonderfully. And if, in the process of aiming your stories at it, you should hit *Argosy, Ghost Stories, Weird Tales* or *Mind Magic*—

Well, what's the obvious answer?

Make a stab at it, anyway; you've got nothing to lose!

* * * * *

Editor's note: The forthcoming Clayton magazine referred to in this article as *Strange Stories,* was actually published under the title *Strange Tales of Mystery and Terror.* Seven issues were printed between September 1931 and January 1933. Most of its fiction was composed by writers known as regular contributors to Weird Tales, including: Clark Ashton Smith, Henry S. Whitehead, August W. Derleth, Jack Williamson, Ray Cummings, Edmond Hamilton, Hugh B. Cave and Robert E. Howard.

Although short-lived, Harry Bates' editing on *Strange Tales of Mystery and Terror* made its fiction as influential on the genre as did the stories in *Weird Tales.*

The cancellation of *Strange Tales of Mystery and Terror* was brought about by the collapse of the entire Clayton Publishing chain due to poor management and rising debt.

A periodical under the title *Strange Stories* did later appear from the Better Publications/The Thrilling Group, in 1940, and published stories on a bi-monthly basis of a similar vein as the earlier weird magazines. It too was short lived and after 13 issues was cancelled.

Mike Chomko, Books

Your source for Altus Press and other fine pulp-related books and periodicals.

Monthly catalog issued.

THE COMPLETE CASES OF
CAPTAIN
SATAN
KING OF DETECTIVES

THE COMPLETE CANALISTIC CASES OF
SEMI DUAL
THE DUAL CASES VOLUME I: 1912

VOLUME 1

THE WHITE SAVAGE
The Complete Tales of Matalaa

MIKE CHOMKO, BOOKS
2217 W. FAIRVIEW STREET
ALLENTOWN, PA 18104-6542
mikechomko@gmail.com
https://sites.google.com/site/mikechomkobooks/

Market Requirements

PSEUDO-SCIENTIFIC MAGAZINES

AMAZING STORIES QUARTERLY, 461 Eighth Avenue, New York City. Dr. T. O'Conor Sloane, Editor. Uses stories built on all the standard pseudo-scientific themes. Overstocked.

ASTOUNDING STORIES, 79 Seventh Avenue, New York City. F. Orlin Tremaine, Editor. Issued monthly; 20 cents a copy; $2.00 a year. Uses science fiction, but it must have a real story and real characters. Lengths are from 3,000 to 6,000 words for shorts; 10,000 to 15,000 words for novelettes. No photographs. Pays one cent a word on acceptance.

FANTASY MAGAZINE, 87-36 162nd Street, Jamaica, Long Island, New York. Mostly staff written. Julius Schwartz, Editor. Does not pay for material.

HORROR STORIES, 205 East 42nd Street, New York City. Rogers Terrill, Editor. Issued monthly; 15 cents a copy. Likes thrilling stories with sheer terror and menace played up. Emphasis on the grewsome. Lengths, 6,500 for shorts; 17,000 words for novels; 10,000 to 12,000 words for novelettes. It is advisable to study the magazine before submitting any material. Pays one cent a word on acceptance.

WEIRD TALES, 840 North Michigan Avenue, Chicago, Illinois. Farnsworth Wright, Editor. Uses weird stories that forecast the marvelous science of the future; tales of other planets, voyages between the worlds; weird and creepy mystery tales; tales of the supernatural, preferably with the logical explanation, etc. Photographs. Pays one cent a word, on publication.

WONDER STORIES, 99 Hudson Street, New York City. Hugo Gernsback, Editor. Issued monthly; 15 cents a copy; $1.50 a year. Wants stories, 1,000 to 100,000 words in length, propounding new, logical scientific theories with original plots, and a minimum of high-toned words. Fantastic though logical development. Stories must be convincing and not fairytalish, hackneyed, or stereotyped. Short shorts should have the O. Henry or surprise ending. While there should be some good science in every story, they do not want pages of technicality—the stories are primarily fiction. No photos. Pays one-half cent a word after publication.

Reprinted from *Writer's Market Annual,* 1936.

Margaret Brundage

"I would submit about three different pencil sketches, and they would make the selection of the one I was to do in color. They chose the scene. Once in a while I would . . . have a friend pose for me. But . . . mostly, it was out of my head. The rate of pay was always $90 per cover."

—Margaret Brundage

ROBERT WEINBERG AND R.A. EVERTS

Margaret Brundage

In a field dominated until just a few years ago by men, Margaret Brundage (1900-1976) was one of the few women to make an indelible mark. She was the leading cover artist for *Weird Tales* during the height of the pulp's popularity and strongly influenced the style and content of the work of many other artists who followed.

Born Margaret Johnson, the artist was a lifelong resident of Chicago. A student early in her life at the Art Institute, she received her formal training at the Chicago Academy of Fine Art but never obtained a degree. She was married in 1927 to Myron Brundage, and a son, Robert, was born in 1929. Her marriage led to her art career since a wandering husband who disappeared for weeks at a time, a baby son, and an invalid mother forced her to work as an agency artist and fashion designer. But the Depression made fashion jobs scarce so she sought magazine work.

The only publishing house with an office in Chicago was *Weird Tales*. Brundage had no knowledge of the contents of the pulp and was not familiar with fantasy or science fiction. However, a Far East female art study in her portfolio caught the eye of Farnsworth Wright, editor of both *Weird Tales* and a companion magazine, *Oriental Stories*. Brundage was signed to paint a cover for the latter magazine. The art proved so popular that Wright gave Brundage a *Weird Tales* cover assignment. Soon she crowded all other artists from the cover of the magazine and became the only woman who was an important science fiction pulp cover artist.

Brundage's earliest covers showed the strong influence of fashion design, featuring a prominent female figure, usually partially clothed, with a vague menace hinted at in the background. She was very good at painting women but was not very good at portraying menaces or monsters. Since she could not afford models, she used magazine photos instead. Farnsworth Wright, picking up on his artist's strong points, soon had the women with less and less clothing, and the erotic aspects of the pictures increased. Even in the pulp magazines of the 1930s, sex sold.

Brundage used pastel chalks for her paintings, and the colors gave her work a soft beauty that was unlike anything else being published in the magazine field. Whereas the powerful covers by Hans Wesso for *Strange Tales* offered supernatural thrills, Brundage's chalk work promised the thrill of beautiful women and unspeakable threats to their virtue.

At first the covers were well received, with many readers writing in enthusiastic praise. However, as the nudes grew bolder, reader sentiment began to change.

This article originally appeared in *A Biographical Dictionary of Science Fiction and Fantasy Artists* by Robert Weinberg, Greenwood Press, 1988, and is reprinted by permission of the author.

When Wright revealed that the covers were being done by a woman, complaints filled the letter column of *Weird Tales:* it was all right to feature nudes on the cover but not nudes that were painted by another woman.

Wright continued to use Brundage despite the complaints. During the height of the Depression, magazines competed bitterly for readers. Cover illustrations sold magazines, and Wright knew that his regulars would buy his publication regardless. Moreover, the nudes attracted one-time buyers who otherwise never would have looked at his magazine.

Several authors, seeing the slant that Brundage covers had taken, made sure that their stories featured at least one scene with a nude woman in jeopardy. Seabury Quinn freely admitted that he aimed his stories for the cover of *Weird Tales* by featuring naked women in his work no matter what the main theme of the tale was. When Virgil Finlay first began illustrating covers for *Weird Tales,* many of his paintings showed a strong Brundage influence. Wright thought that Brundage-style nudes sold his magazine, and no matter who did the cover, the illustration had to remain the same.

When *Weird Tales* was sold in late 1938 and its editorial offices moved to New York City, Brundage found herself without a job. Her pastel paintings had to be kept under glass at all times, and shipping glass to New York was expen-

Spring 1932

sive. In addition, Brundage used to visit Wright at his office every week to discuss cover ideas, but now editor and artist conferences were impossible. Therefore, Virgil Finlay, who lived on the East Coast, took over cover assignments for *Weird Tales.*

Brundage found little market in Chicago for her pastel nudes and left the fantasy art field, although she did sell a few more paintings to *Weird Tales* in the 1940s. By this time she was divorced from her husband and was forced to take various low-paying art jobs. Forgotten by most science fiction and fantasy fans, she died in near poverty after a long illness.

Brundage's nudes brought sex to the covers of science fiction and fantasy magazines. Most covers before hers had featured either giant machinery, spaceships, or monsters. Brundage's work proved that the same type of cover that sold many other pulp magazines would also work for the SF fantasy lines. She was the first of many artists to become known for women-in-peril-style covers.

July 1933

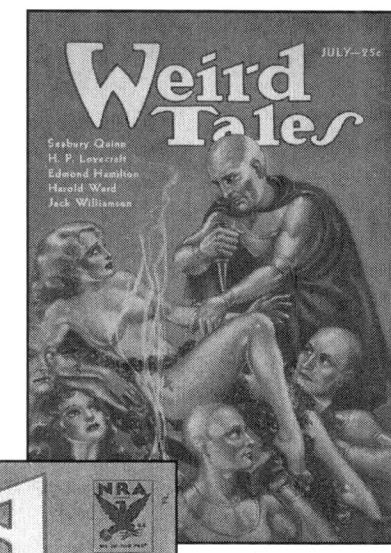

October 1933
One of the most reproduced covers
Brundage provided for *Weird Tales*.

November 1934

In his book, *Weird Tales,* chronicling
the history of the magazine, author
Alistair Durie labeled this Brundage
outing as a "delicious cover."

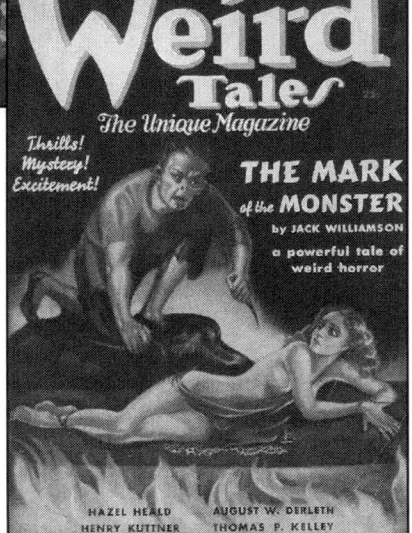

May 1937

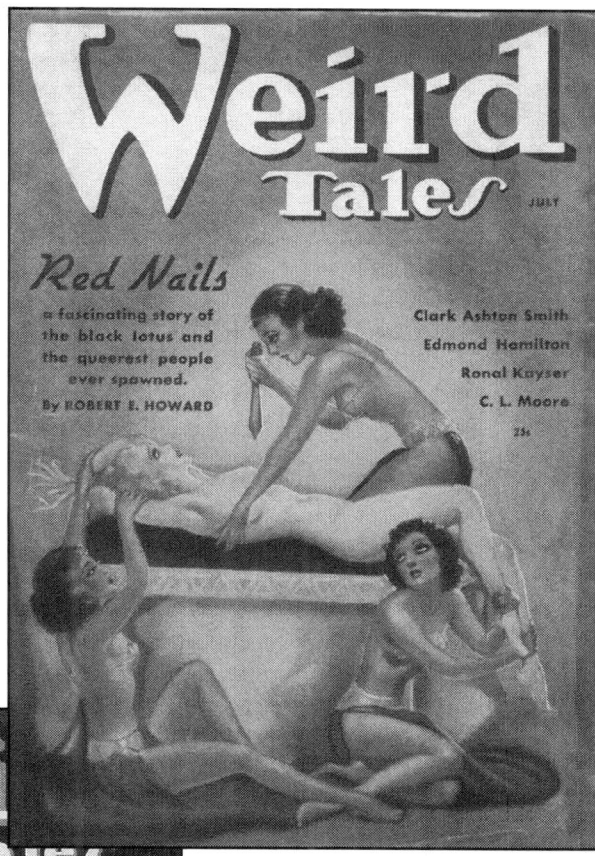

July 1936. Cover story for the
Conan novella, "Red Nails"
by Robert E. Howard,
the last Conan story
submitted prior to
Howard's death.

January 1937

January 1936

January 1938

June 1939

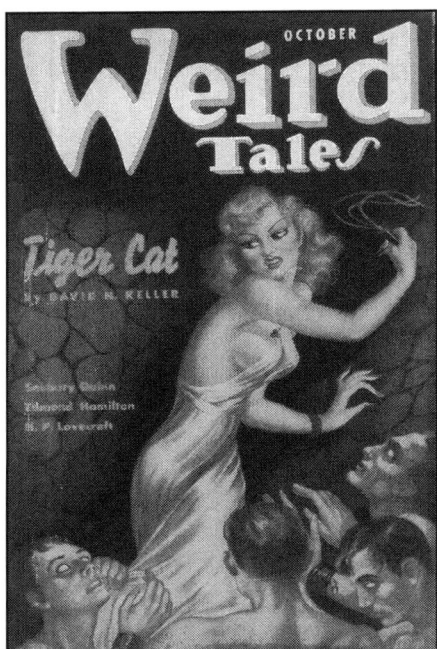

October 1937

Girl Model Parade, No. 8 (1939).

Editor's note: Seeking to replace her *Weird Tales* market after their offices relocated to New York, Brundage sought work in the late 1930s from other Chicago-based publishers, including Sun Publications. Sun published the historical adventure pulp, *Golden Fleece,* but also published "artists" magazines. These featured nude photos which were intended to be used purely for artistic reference. One of their stable was *Girl Model Parade.* In issue No. 8, five illustrations by Brundage appeared, based on five photos running adjacent to them, thereby serving as examples of how an artist might use these photos in their own work. As best as research allows, these rare images, from a little known and little documented period of Brundage's career, have not been reproduced since their 1939 publication.

Girl Model Parade, No. 8 (1939).

Girl Model Parade, No. 8 (1939).

Girl Model Parade, No. 8 (1939).

Girl Model Parade, No. 8 (1939).

SPECIAL ANNOUNCEMENT

New auctions coming soon, with thousands of pulps coming to the market. A near set of ADVENTURE, a set of WEIRD TALES, plus thousands of detective, spicy, hero and more coming to our auction site soon.

As the number one pulp auction site in the world, our services have never been in higher demand. Each item passes through our hands, graded and scanned, assuring you...the collector...of a worry free auction experience.

Our auction site reflects our desire to make your purchases with as little hassle as possible. Where else can you find an auction company that only charges a nominal 10% buyers premium? How about an auction site that resembles a standard online auction, but won't allow someone to snipe your prized collectable. Any item that receives a bid with less than a minute, will automatically be extended an additional 3 minutes to counter bids. Our site more closely resembles a live auction than that of a standard online auction site.

Keep an eye on our auction site for upcoming auctions, as we are working diligently on preparing nearly 8000 more books for auction.

CATALOGS and FULL COLOR BOOKS of these great collectibles will be available soon.

Adventure House - 914 Laredo Rd - Silver Spring, MD 20901
www.adventurehouse.com - gunnison@adventurehouse.com

Editor's note: The cover for the first issue of *Weird Tales* has been an oft-reprinted image, reproduced in dozen of pulp-related retrospectives and histories. But how many have actually read the title story from it?

With this thought in mind, "Ooze" by Anthony M. Rud, from *Weird Tales, Vol. 1. No.1, March 1923,* was selected for inclusion in this volume.

Additionally, this story, with not only its weird, but its scientific overtones, nicely ties together both of these genre-type magazines for its anniversary recognition.

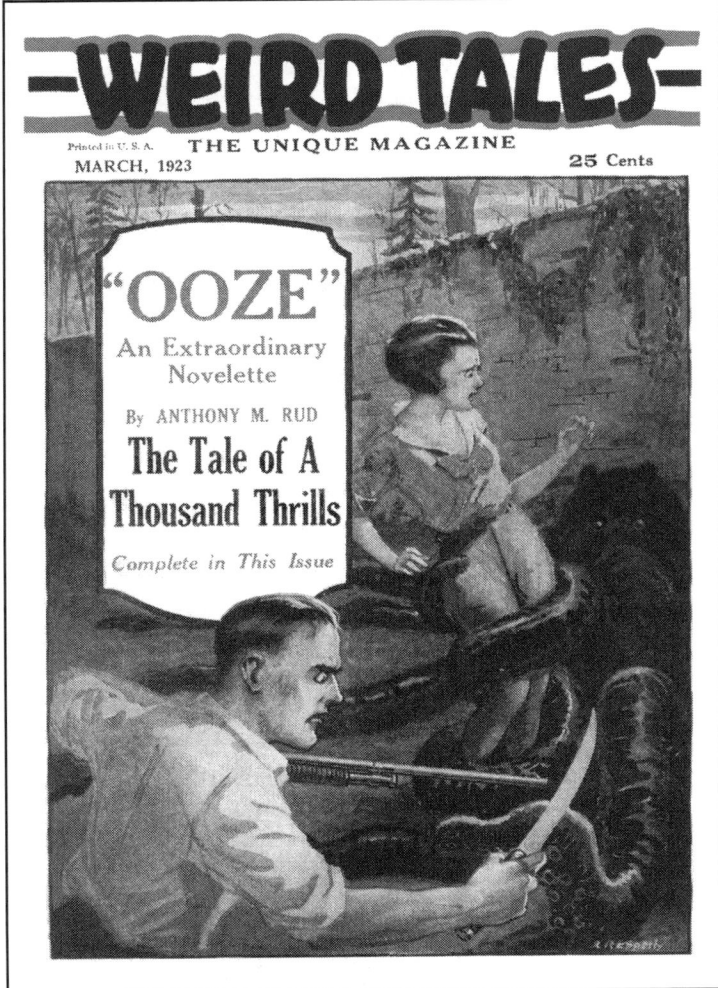

Cover art by R.R. Epperly

Ooze

ANTHONY M. RUD

I

In the heart of a second-growth piney-woods jungle of southern Alabama, a region sparsely settled save by backwoods blacks and Cajuns—that queer, half-wild people descended from Acadian exiles of the middle eighteenth century—stands a strange, enormous ruin.

Interminable trailers of Cherokee rose, white-laden during a single month of spring, have climbed the heights of its three remaining walls. Palmetto fans rise knee high above the base. A dozen scattered live oaks, now belying their nomenclature because of choking tufts of gray, Spanish moss and two-foot circlets of mistletoe parasite that have stripped bare of foliage the gnarled, knotted limbs, lean fantastic beards against the crumbling brick.

Immediately beyond, where the ground becomes soggier and lower—dropping away hopelessly into the tangle of dogwood, holly, poison sumac and pitcher plants that is Moccasin Swamp—undergrowth of ti-ti and annis has formed a protecting wall impenetrable to all save the furtive ones. Some few outcasts utilize the stinking depths of that sinister swamp, distilling "shinny" or "pure cawn" liquor for illicit trade.

Tradition states that this is the case, at least—a tradition which antedates that of the premature ruin by many decades. I believe it, for during evenings intervening between investigations of the awesome spot I often was approached as a possible customer by wood-billies who could not fathom how anyone dared venture near without plenteous fortification of liquid courage.

I knew "shinny," therefore I did not purchase it for personal consumption. A dozen times I bought a quart or two, merely to establish credit among the Cajuns, pouring away the vile stuff immediately into the sodden ground. It seemed then that only through filtration and condensation of their dozens of weird tales regarding "Daid House" could I arrive at understanding of the mystery and weight of horror hanging about the place.

Certain it is that out of all the superstitious cautioning, head-wagging and whispered nonsensities I obtained only two indisputable facts. The first was that no money, and no supporting battery of ten-gauge shotguns loaded with filled shot, could induce either Cajun or darky of the region to approach within five hundred yards of that flowering wall! The second fact I shall dwell upon later.

Perhaps it would be as well, as I am only a mouthpiece in this chronicle, to relate in brief why I came to Alabama on this mission.

I am a scribbler of general fact articles, no fiction writer as was Lee Cranmar—though doubtless the confession is superfluous. Lee was my roommate during college days. I knew his family well, admiring John Corliss Cranmer even more than I admired the son and friend—and almost as much as Peggy Breede whom Lee married. Peggy liked me, but that was all. I cherish sanctified memory of her for just that much, as no other woman before or since has granted this gangling dyspeptic even a hint of joyous and sorrowful intimacy.

Work kept me to the city. Lee, on the other hand, coming of wealthy family—and, from the first, earning from his short stories and novel royalties more than I wrested from editorial coffer—needed no anchorage. He and Peggy honeymooned a four-month trip to Alaska, visited Honolulu next winter, fished for salmon on Cain's River, New Brunswick, and generally enjoyed the outdoors at all seasons.

They kept an apartment in Wilmette, near Chicago, yet during the few spring and fall seasons they were "home," both preferred to rent a suite at one of the country clubs to which Lee belonged. I suppose they spent thrice or five times the amount Lee actually earned, yet, for my part, I only honored that the two should find such great happiness in life and still accomplish artistic triumph.

They were honest, zestful young Americans, the type—and pretty nearly the *only* type—two million dollars cannot spoil. John Corliss Cranmer, father of Lee, though as different from his boy as a microscope is different from a painting by Remington, was even further from being dollar conscious. He lived in a world bounded only by the widening horizon of biological science—and his love for the two who would carry on that Cranmer name.

Many a time I used to wonder how it could be that as gentle, clean-souled and lovable a gentleman as John Corliss Cranmer could have ventured so far into scientific research without attaining small-caliber atheism. Few do. He believed both in God and human kind. To accuse him of murdering his boy and the girl wife who had come to be loved as the mother of baby Elsie—as well as blood and flesh of his own family—was a gruesome, terrible absurdity! Yes, even when John Corliss Cranmer was declared unmistakably insane!

Lacking a relative in the world, baby Elsie was given to me—and the middle-aged couple who had accompanied the three as servants about half of the known world. Elsie would be Peggy over again. I worshiped her, knowing that if my stewardship of her interests could make of her a woman of Peggy's loveliness and worth I should not have lived in vain. And at four Elsie stretched out her arms to me after vain attempt to jerk out the bobbed tail of Lord Dick, my tolerant old Airedale—and called me "papa."

I felt a deep-down choking . . . yes, those strangely long black lashes some day might droop in fun or coquetry, but now baby Elsie held wistful, trusting seriousness in depths of ultramarine eyes—that same seriousness which only Lee had brought to Peggy.

Responsibility in one instant became double. That she might come to love me as more than foster parent was my dearest wish. Still, through selfishness I could not rob her of rightful heritage; she must know in after years. And the tale that I would tell her must not be the horrible suspicion which had been bandied about in common talk!

I went to Alabama, leaving Elsie in the competent hands of Mrs. Daniels and her husband, who had helped care for her since birth.

In my possession, prior to the trip, were the scant facts known to authorities at the time of John Corliss Cranmer's escape and disappearance. They were incredible enough.

For conducting biological research upon forms of protozon life, John Corliss Cranmer had hit upon this region of Alabama. Near a great swamp teeming with microscopic organisms, and situated in a semi-tropical belt where freezing weather rarely intruded to harden the bogs, the spot seemed ideal for his purpose.

Through Mobile he could secure supplies daily by truck. The isolation suited. With only an octoroon man to act as chef, houseman and valet for the times he entertained no visitors, he brought down scientific apparatus, occupying temporary quarters in the village of Burdett's Corners while his woods house was in process of construction.

By all accounts the Lodge, as he termed it, was a substantial affair of eight or nine rooms, built of logs and planed lumber bought at Oak Grove. Lee and Peggy were expected to spend a portion of each year with him; quail, wild turkey and deer abounded, which fact made such a vacation certain to please the pair. At other times all save four rooms was closed.

This was in 1907, the year of Lee's marriage. Six years later, when I came down, no sign of a house remained except certain mangled and rotting timbers projecting from viscid soil—or what seemed like soil. And a twelve-foot wall of brick had been built to enclose the house completely! One portion of this had fallen *inward!*

II

I wasted weeks of time at first, interviewing officials of the police department at Mobile, the town marshals and county sheriffs of Washington and Mobile counties, and officials of the psychopathic hospital from which Cranmer made his escape.

In substance the story was one of baseless homicidal mania. Cranmer the elder had been away until late fall, attending two scientific conferences in the North, and then going abroad to compare certain of his findings with those of a Dr. Gemmler of Prague University. Unfortunately, Gemmler was assassinated by a religious fanatic shortly afterward. The fanatic voiced virulent objection to all Mendelian research as blasphemous. This was his only defense. He was hanged.

Search of Gemmler's notes and effects revealed nothing save an immense amount of laboratory data on *karyokinesis*—the process of chromosome arrangement occurring in first growing cells of higher animal embryos. Apparently Cranmer had hoped to develop some similarities, or point out differences between hereditary factors occurring in lower forms of life and those half-demonstrated in the cat and monkey. The authorities had found nothing that helped me. Cranmer had gone crazy; was that not sufficient explanation?

Perhaps it was for them, but not for me—and Elsie.

But to the slim basis of fact I was able to unearth:

No one wondered when a fortnight passed without appearance of any person from the Lodge. Why should anyone worry? A provision salesman in Mobile called up twice, but failed to complete a connection. He merely shrugged. The Cranmers had gone away somewhere on a trip. In a week, a month, a year they would be back. Meanwhile he lost commissions, but what of it? He had no responsibility for these queer nuts up there in the piney-woods. Crazy? Of course! Why should any guy with millions to spend shut himself up among the Cajuns and draw microscope-enlarged notebook pictures of—what the salesman called—"germs?"

A stir was aroused at the end of the fortnight, but the commotion confined itself to building circles. Twenty carloads of building brick, fifty bricklayers, and a quarter-acre of fine-meshed wire—the sort used for screening off pens of rodents and small marsupials in a zoological garden—were ordered, *damn expense, hurry!* by an unshaved, tattered man who identified himself with difficulty as John Corliss Cranmer.

He looked strange, even then. A certified check for the total amount, given in advance, and another check of absurd size slung toward a labor *entrepreneur,* silenced objection, however. These millionaires were apt to be flighty. When they wanted something they wanted it at the tap of the bell. Well, why not drag down the big profits? A poorer man would have been jacked up in a day. Cranmer's fluid gold bathed him in immunity to criticism.

The encircling wall was built, and roofed with wire netting that drooped about the squat-pitch of the Lodge. Curious inquiries of workmen went unanswered until the final day.

Then Cranmer, a strange, intense apparition who showed himself more shabby than a quay derelict, assembled every manjack of the workmen. In one hand he grasped a wad of blue slips—fifty-six of them. In the other he held a Luger automatic.

"I offer each man a thousand dollars for *silence!*" he announced. "As an alternative—*death!* You know little. Will all of you consent to swear upon your honor that nothing which has occurred here will be mentioned elsewhere? By this I mean *absolute* silence! You will not come back here to investigate anything. You will not tell your wives. You will not open your mouths even upon the witness stand in case you are called! My price is one thousand apiece.

"In case one of you betrays me, *I give you my word that this man shall die!* I am rich. I can hire men to do murder. Well, what do you say?"

The men glanced apprehensively about. The threatening Luger decide them. To a man they accepted the blue slips—and, save for one witness who lost all sense of fear and morality in drink, none of the fifty-six has broken his pledge, as far as I know. That one bricklayer died later in delirium tremens.

It might have been different had not John Corliss Cranmer escaped.

III

They found him the first time, mouthing meaningless phrases concerning an amoeba—one of the tiny forms of protoplasmic life he was known to have studied. Also he leaped into a hysteria of self-accusation. He had murdered two innocent people! The tragedy was his crime. He had drowned them in ooze! Ah, God!

Unfortunately for all concerned, Cranmer, dazed and indubitably stark insane, chose to perform a strange travesty on fishing four miles to the west of his lodge—on the further border of Moccasin Swamp. His clothing had been torn to shreds, his hat was gone, and he was coated from head to foot with gluey mire. It was far from strange that the good folk of Shanksville, who never had glimpsed the eccentric millionaire, failed to associate him with Cranmer.

They took him in, searched his pockets—finding no sign save an inordinate sum of money—and then put him under medical care. Two precious weeks elapsed before Dr. Quirk reluctantly acknowledged that he could do nothing more for this patient, and notified the proper authorities.

Then much more time was wasted. Hot April and half of still hotter May passed by before the loose ends were connected. Then it did little good to know that this raving unfortunate was Cranmer, or that the two persons of whom he shouted in disconnected delirium actually had disappeared. Alienists absolved him of responsibility. He was confined in a cell reserved for the violent.

Meanwhile, strange things occurred back at the Lodge—which now, for good and sufficient reason, was becoming known to dwellers of the woods as Dead House. Until one of the walls fell in, however, there had been no chance to see— unless one possessed the temerity to climb either one of the tall live oaks, or mount the barrier itself. No doors or opening of any sort had been placed in that hastily constructed wall!

By the time the western side of the wall fell, not a native for miles around but feared the spot far more than even the bottomless, snake-infested bogs that lay to west and north.

The single statement was all John Corliss Cranmer ever gave to the world. It proved sufficient. An immediate search was instituted. It showed that less than three weeks before the day of initial reckoning, his son and Peggy had come to visit him for the second time that winter—leaving Elsie behind in company of the Daniels pair. They had rented a pair of Gordons for quail hunting, and had gone out. That was the last anyone had seen of them.

The backwoods Negro who glimpsed them stalking a covey behind their two pointing dogs had known no more—even when sweated through twelve hours of third degree. Certain suspicious circumstances (having to do only with his regular pursuit of "shinny" transportation) had caused him to fall under suspicioun at first. He was dropped.

Two days later the scientist himself was apprehended—a gibbering idiot who sloughed his pole—holding on to the baited hook—into a marsh where nothing save moccasins, an errant alligator, or amphibian life could have been snared.

His mind was three-quarters dead. Cranmer then was in the state of the dope fiend who rouses to a sitting position to ask seriously how many Bolshevists were killed by Julius Caesar before he was stabbed by Brutus, or why it was that Roller canaries sang only on Wednesday evenings. He knew that tragedy of the most sinister sort had stalked through his life—but little more, at first.

Later the police obtained that one statement that he had murdered two human beings, but never could means or motive be established. Official guess as to the means was no more than wild conjecture; it mentioned enticing the victims to the noisome depths of Moccasin Swamp, there to let them flounder and sink.

The two were his son and daughter in-law, Lee and Peggy!

IV

By feigning coma—then awakening with suddenness to assault three attendants with incredible ferocity and strength—John Corliss Cranmer escaped from Elizabeth Ritter Hospital.

How he hid, how he managed to traverse sixty-odd intervening miles and still balk detection, remains a minor mystery to be explained only by the assumption that maniacal cunning sufficed to outwit saner intellects.

Traverse these miles he did, though until I was fortunate enough to uncover evidence to this effect, it was supposed generally that he had made his escape as stowaway on one of the banana boats or had buried himself in some portion of the nearer woods where he was unknown. The truth ought to be welcome to householders of Shanksville. Burdett's Corners and vicinage—those excusably prudent ones who to this day keep loaded shotguns handy and barricade their doors at nightfall.

The first ten days of my investigation may be touched upon in brief. I made headquarters in Burdett's Corners, and drove out each morning, carrying lunch and returning for my grits and piney-woods pork or mutton before nightfall. My first plan had been to camp out at the edge of the swamp, for opportunity to enjoy the outdoors comes rarely in my direction. Yet after one cursory examination of the premises I abandoned the idea. I did not *want* to camp alone there. And I am less superstitious than a real estate agent.

It was, perhaps, psychic warning; more probably the queer, faint, salty odor as of fish left to decay, which hung about the ruin, made too unpleasant an impression upon my olfactory sense. I experienced a distinct chill every time the lengthening shadows caught me near Dead House.

The smell impressed me. In newspaper reports of the case one ingenious explanation had been worked out. To the rear of the spot where Dead House had stood—inside the wall—was a swampy hollow circular in shape. Only a little real mud lay in the bottom of the bowl-like depression now, but one reporter on the staff of *The Mobile Register* guessed that during the tenancy of the lodge it had been a fish pool. Drying up of the water had killed the fish, who now permeated the remnant of mud with this foul odor.

The possibility that Cranmer had needed to keep fresh fish at hand for some of his experiments silenced the natural objection that in a country where every stream holds gar pike, bass, catfish and many other edible varieties, no one would dream of stocking a stagnant puddle.

After tramping about the enclosure, testing the queerly brittle, desiccated top stratum of earth within and speculating concerning the possible purpose of the wall, I cut off a long limb of chinaberry and probed the mud. One fragment of fish spine would confirm the guess of that imaginative reporter.

I found nothing resembling a piscal skeleton, but established several facts. First, this mud crater had definite bottom only three or four feet below the surface of remaining ooze. Second, the fishy stench became stronger as I stirred. Third, at one time the mud, water, or whatever had comprised the balance of content, had reached the rim of the bowl. The last showed by certain marks plain enough when the crusty, two-inch stratum of upper coating was broken away. It was puzzling.

The nature of that thin, desiccated effluvium which seemed to cover every-thing even to the lower foot or two of brick, came in for next inspection. It was strange stuff, unlike any earth I ever had seen, though undoubtedly some form of scum drained in from the swamp at the time of river floods or cloudbursts (which in this section are common enough in spring and fall). It crumbled beneath the fingers. When I walked over it, the stuff crunched hollowly. In fainter degree it possessed the fishy odor also.

I took some samples where it lay thickest upon the ground, and also a few where there seemed to be no more than a depth of a sheet of paper. Later I would have a laboratory analysis made.

Apart from any possible bearing the stuff might have upon the disappearance of my three friends, I felt the tug of article interest—that wonder over anything strange or seemingly inexplicable which lends the hunt for fact a certain glamour and romance all its own. To myself I was going to have to explain sooner or later just why this layer covered the entire space within the walls and was not percep-tible *anywhere* outside! The enigma could wait, however—or so I decided.

Far more interesting were the traces of violence apparent on wall and what once had been a house. The latter seemed to have been ripped from its foundations by a giant hand, crushed out of semblance to a dwelling, and then cast in frag-ments about the base of wall—mainly on the south side, where heaps of twisted, broken timbers lay in profusion. On the opposite side there had been such heaps once, but now only charred sticks, coated with that gray-black, omnipresent coat of dessication, remained. These piles of charcoal had been sifted and examined most carefully by the authorities, as one theory had been advanced that Cranmer had burned the bodies of his victims. Yet no sign whatever of human remains was discovered.

The fire, however, pointed out one odd fact that controverted the reconstruc-tions made by detectives months before. The latter, suggesting the dried scum to have drained in from the swamp, believed that the house timbers had floated out to the sides of the wall—there to arrange themselves in a series of piles! The absurdity of such a theory showed even more plainly in the fact that if the scum had filtered through in such a flood, the timbers most certainly had been dragged into piles *previously!* Some had burned—*and the scum coated their charred sur-faces!*

What had been the force that had torn the lodge to bits as if in spiteful fury? Why had the parts of the wreckage been burned, the rest to escape?

Right here I felt was the keynote to the mystery, yet I could imagine no explanation. That John Corliss Cranmer himself—physically sound, yet a man who for decades had led a sedentary life—could have accomplished such destruction, unaided, was difficult to believe.

V

I turned, my attention to the wall, hoping for evidence which might suggest another theory.

That wall had been an example of the worst snide construction. Though little more than a year old, the parts left standing showed evidence that they had begun to decay the day the last brick was laid. The mortar had fallen from the interstices. Here and there a brick had cracked and dropped out. Fibrils of the climbing vines had penetrated crevices, working for early destruction.

And one side already had fallen.

It was here that the first glimmering suspicion of the terrible truth was forced upon me. The scattered bricks, even those which had rolled inward toward the gaping foundation lodge, *had not been coated with scum!* This was curious, yet it could be explained by surmise that the flood itself had undermined this weakest portion of the wall. I cleared away a mass of brick from the spot on which the structure had stood; to my surprise I found it exceptionally firm! Hard red clay lay beneath! The flood conception was faulty; only some great force, exerted from inside or outside, could have wreaked such destruction.

When careful measurement, analysis and deduction convinced me—mainly from the fact that the lowermost layers of brick all had fallen *outward,* while the upper portions toppled *in*—I began to link up this mysterious and horrific force with the one which had rent the Lodge asunder. It looked as though a typhoon or gigantic centrifuge had needed elbow room in ripping down the wooden structure.

But I got nowhere with the theory, though in ordinary affairs I am called a man of too great imaginative tendencies. No less than three editors have cautioned me on this point. Perhaps it was the narrowing influence of great personal sympathy—yes, and love. I make no excuses though beyond a dim understanding at some terrific, implacable force must have made this spot his playground, I ended my ninth day of notetaking and investigation almost as much in the dark as I had been while a thousand miles away in Chicago.

Then I started among the darkies and Cajuns. A whole day I listened to yarns of the days which preceded Cranmer's escape from Elizabeth Ritter Hospital—days in which furtive men sniffed poisoned air for miles around Dead House, finding the odor intolerable. Days in which it seemed none possessed nerve enough to approach close. Days when the most fanciful tales of medieval superstitions were spun. These tales I shall not give; the truth is incredible enough.

At noon upon the eleventh day I chanced upon Rori Pailleron, a Cajun—and one of the least prepossessing of all with whom I had come in contact. "Chanced" perhaps is a bad word. I had listed every dweller of the woods within a five-mile radius. Rori was sixteenth on my list. I went to him only after interviewing all four of the Crabiers and two whole families of Pichons. And Rori regarded me with the utmost suspicion until I made him a present of the two quarts of "shinny" purchased of the Pichons.

Because long practice has perfected me in the technique of seeming to drink another man's awful liquor—no, I'm not an absolute prohibitionist; fine wine or twelve-year-in-cask Bourbon whisky arouses my definite interest—I fooled Pailleron from the start. I shall omit preliminaries, and leap to the first admission from him that he knew more concerning Dead House and its former inmates than any of the other darkies or Cajuns roundabout.

". . . But I ain't talkin'. *Sacre!* If I should open my gab, what might fly out? It is for keeping silent, y'r damn' right! . . ."

I agreed. He was a wise man—educated to some extent in the queer schools and churches maintained exclusively by Cajuns in the depths of the wood yet naive withal.

We drank. And I never had to ask another leading question. The liquor made him want to interest me, and the only extraordinary topic in this whole neck of the woods was the Dead House.

Three-quarters of a pint of acrid, nauseous fluid, and he hinted darkly. A pint, and he told me something I scarcely could believe. Another half pint . . . But I shall give his confession in condensed form.

He had known Joe Sibley, the octoroon chef, houseman and valet who served Cranmer. Through Joe, Rori had furnished certain indispensables in the way of food to the Cranmer household. At first, these salable articles had been exclusively vegetable—white and yellow turnip, sweet potatoes, corn and beans—but later, *meat!*

Yes, meat especially—whole lambs, slaughtered and quartered, the coarsest variety of piney-woods pork and beef, all in immense quantity!

VI

In December of the fatal winter Lee and his wife stopped down at the Lodge for ten days or thereabouts.

They were en route to Cuba at the time, intending to be away five or six weeks. Their original plan had been only to wait over a day or so in the piney-woods, but something caused an amendment to the scheme.

The two dallied. Lee seemed to have become vastly absorbed in something—so much absorbed that it was only when Peggy insisted upon continuing their trip, that he could tear himself away.

It was during those ten days that he began buying meat. Meager bits of it at first—rabbit, a pair of squirrels, or perhaps a few quail beyond the number he and Peggy shot. Rori furnished the game, thinking nothing of it except that Lee paid double prices—and insisted upon keeping the purchases secret from other members of the household.

"I'm putting it across on the Governor, Rori!" he said once with wink. "Going to give him the shock of his life. So you mustn't let on, even to Joe about what I want you to do. Maybe it won't work out, but if it does . . .! Dad'll have the scientific world at his feet! He doesn't blow his own horn anywhere near enough, you know."

Rori didn't know. Hadn't a suspicion what Lee was talking about. Still, if this rich, young idiot wanted to pay him a half dollar in good silver coin for a quail that anyone—himself included—could knock down with a five-cent shell, Rori was well satisfied to keep his mouth shut. Each evening he brought some of the small game. And each day Lee Cranmer seemed to have use for an additional quail or so . . .

When he was ready to leave for Cuba, Lee came forward with the strangest of propositions. He fairly whispered vehemence and desire for secrecy! He would tell Rori, and would pay the Cajun five hundred dollars—half in advance, and half at the end of five weeks when Lee himself would return from Cuba—provided Rori agreed to adhere absolutely to a certain secret program! The money was more than a fortune to Rori; it was undreamt-of affluence. The Cajun acceded.

"He wuz tellin' me then how the ol' man had raised some kind of pet," Rori confided, "an' wanted to get shet of it. So he give it to Lee, tellin' him to kill it, but Lee was sot on foolin' him. W'at I ask yer is, w'at kind of a pet is it w'at lives down in a mud sink *an' eats a couple hawgs every night?*"

I couldn't imagine, so I pressed him for further details. Here at last was something that sounded like a clue!

He really knew too little. The agreement with Lee provided that if Rori carried out the provisions exactly, he should be paid extra and his exorbitant scale of all additional outlay, when Lee returned.

The young man gave him a daily schedule that Rori showed. Each evening he was to procure, slaughter and cut up a definite—and growing—amount of meat. Every item was checked, and I saw that they ran from five pounds up to *forty!*

"What in Heaven's name, did you do with it?" I demanded, excited now and pouring him an additional drink for fear caution might return to him.

"Took it through the bushes in back an' slung it in the mud sink there! An' suthin' come up an' drug it down!"

"A gator?"

"*Diable!* How should I know? It was dark. I wouldn't go close." He shuddered, and the fingers that lifted his glass shook as with sudden chill. "Mebbe you'd of done it, huh? Not *me,* though! The young fellah tole me to sling it in, an I slung it.

"A couple times I come around in the light, but there wasn't nuthin' there you could see. Jes' mud, an' some water. Mebbe the thing didn't come out in daytimes. . . ."

"Perhaps not," I agreed, straining every mental resource to imagine what Lee's sinister pet could have been. "But you said something about *two hogs a day?* What did you mean by that? This paper, proof enough that you're telling the truth so far, states that on the thirty-fifth day you were to throw forty pounds of meat—any kind—into the sink. Two hogs, even the piney woods variety, weigh a lot more than forty pounds!"

"Them was after—after he come back!"

From this point onward, Rori's tale became more and more enmeshed in the vagaries induced by bad liquor. His tongue thickened. I shall give his story without attempt to reproduce further verbal barbarities, or the occasional prodding I had to give in order to keep him from maundering into foolish jargon.

Lee had paid munificently. His only objection to the manner in which Rori had carried out his orders was that the orders themselves had been deficient. The pet, he said had grown enormously. It was hungry, ravenous. Lee himself had supplemented the fare with huge pails of scraps from the kitchen.

From that day Lee purchased from Rori whole sheep and hogs! The Cajun continued to bring the carcasses at nightfall, but no longer did Lee permit him to approach the pool. The young man appeared chronically excited now. He had a tremendous secret—one the extent of which even his father did not guess, and one that would astonish the world! Only a week or two more and he would spring it. First he would have to arrange certain data.

Then came the day when everyone disappeared from Dead House. Rori came around several times, but concluded that all of the occupants had folded tents and departed—doubtless taking their mysterious "pet" along. Only when he saw from a distance, Joe, the octoroon servant, returning along the road on foot toward the Lodge, did his slow mental processes begin to ferment. That afternoon Rori visited the strange place for the next to last time.

He did not go to the Lodge itself—and there were reasons. While still some hundreds of yards away from the place, a terrible, sustained screaming reached his ears! It was faint, yet unmistakably the voice of Joe! Throwing a pair of number two shells into the breach of his shotgun, Rori hurried on, taking his usual path through the brush at the back.

He saw—and as he told me even "shinny" drunkenness fled his chattering tones—Joe, the octoroon. Aye, he stood in the yard, far from the pool into which Rori had thrown the carcasses—*and Joe could not move!*

Rori failed to explain in full, but something, a slimy, amorphous something which glistened in the sunlight, already had engulfed the man to his shoulders! Breath was cut off. Joe's contorted face writhed with horror and beginning suffocation. One hand—all that was free of the rest of him!—beat feebly upon the rubbery, translucent thing that was engulfing his body!

Then Joe sank from sight . . .

VII

Five days of liquored indulgence passed before Rori, alone in his shaky cabin, convinced himself that he had seen a fantasy born of alcohol. He came back the last time—to find a high wall of brick surrounding the Lodge, and including the pool of mud into which he had thrown the meat!

While he hesitated, circling the place without discovering an opening which he would not have dared to use, even had he found it—a crashing, tearing of timbers, and persistent sound of awesome destruction came from within. He swung himself into one of the oaks near the wall. And he was just in time to see the last supporting stanchions of the Lodge give way *outward!*

The whole structure came apart. The roof fell in—yet seemed to move after it had fallen. Logs of wall deserted retaining grasp of their spikes like layers of plywood in the grasp of the shearing machine!

That was all. Soddenly intoxicated now, Rori mumbled more phrases, giving me the idea that on another day when he became sober once more, he might add to his statements, but I—numbed to the soul—scarcely cared. If that which he related was true, what nightmare of madness must have been consumated here!

I could vision some things now that concerned Lee and Peggy, horrible things. Only remembrance of Elsie kept me faced forward in the search—for now it seemed almost that the handiwork of a madman must be preferred to what Rori claimed to have seen! What had been that sinister, translucent thing? That glistening thing which lumped upward about a man, smothering, engulfing?

Queerly enough, though such a theory as came most easily to mind now would have outraged reason in me if suggested concerning total strangers, I asked myself only what details of Rori's revelation had been exaggerated by fright and fumes of liquor. And as I sat on the creaking bench in his cabin, staring unseeing as he lurched down to the floor, fumbling with a lock box of green tin that lay under his cot, and muttering, the answer to all my questions lay within reach!

It was not until next day, however, that I made the discovery. Heavy of heart I had reexamined the spot where the Lodge had stood, then made my way to the Cajun's cabin again, seeking sober confirmation of what he had told me during intoxication.

In imagining that such a spree for Rori would be ended by a single night, however, I was mistaken. He lay sprawled almost as I had left him. Only two factors were changed. No "shinny" was left and lying open, with its miscellaneous contents strewed about, was the tin box. Rori somehow had managed to open it with the tiny key still clutched in his hand.

Concern for his safety alone was what made me notice the box. It was a receptacle for small fishing tackle of the sort carried here and there by any sportsman. Tangles of Dowagiac minnows, spoon hooks ranging in size to silver-backed number eights; three reels still carrying line of different weights, spinners, casting plugs, wobblers, floating baits, were spilled out upon the rough plank flooring where they might snag Rori badly if he rolled. I gathered them, intending to save him an accident.

With the miscellaneous assortment in my hands, however, I stopped dead. Something had caught my eye—something lying flush with the bottom of the lock box! I stared, and then swiftly tossed the hooks and other impedimenta upon the table. What I had glimpsed there in the box was a looseleaf notebook of the sort used for recording laboratory data! And Rori scarcely could read, let alone *write!*

Feverishly, a riot of recognition, surmise, hope and fear bubbling in my brain, I grabbed the book and threw it open. At once I knew that this was the end. The pages were scribbled in pencil, but the handwriting was that precise chirography I knew as belonging to John Corliss Cranmer, the scientist!

> *" . . . Could he not have obeyed my instructions! Oh, God! This . . ."*

These were the words at top of the first page that met my eye.

Because knowledge of the circumstances, the relation of which I pried out of the reluctant Rori only some days later when I had him in Mobile as a police witness for the sake of my friend's vindication, is necessary to understanding, I shall interpolate.

Rori had not told me everything. On his late visit to the vicinage of Dead House he saw more. A crouching figure, seated Turk fashion on top of the wall, appeared to be writing industriously. Rori recognized the man as Cranmer, yet did not hail him. He had no opportunity.

Just as the Cajun came near, Cranmer rose, thrust the notebook, which had rested across his knees, into the box. Then he turned, tossed outside the wall both the locked box and a ribbon to which was attached the key.

Then his arms raised toward heaven. For five seconds he seemed to invoke the mercy of Power beyond all of man's scientific prying. And finally he leaped, *inside . . . !*

Rori did not climb to investigate. He knew that directly below this portion of wall lay the mud sink into which he had thrown the chunks of meat!

VIII

This is a true transcription of the statement I inscribed, telling the sequence of actual events at Dead House. The original of the statement now lies in the archives of the detective department.

Cranmer's notebook, though written in a precise hand, yet betrayed the man's insanity by incoherence and frequent repetitions. My statement has been accepted now, both by alienists and by detectives who had entertained different theories in respect to the case. It quashes the noisome hints and suspicions regarding three of the finest Americans who ever lived—and also one queer supposition dealing with supposed criminal tendencies in poor Joe, the octoroon.

John Corliss Cranmer *went* insane for sufficient cause!

As readers of popular fiction know well, Lee Cranmer's forte was the writing of what is called—among fellows in the craft—the pseudo-scientific story. In plain words, this means a yarn, based upon solid fact in the field of astronomy, chemistry, anthropology or whatnot, which carries to logical conclusion unproved theories of men who devote their lives to searching out further nadirs of fact.

In certain fashion these men are allies of science. Often they visualize something which has not been imagined even by the best of men from whom they secure data, thus opening new horizons of possibility. In a large way Jules Verne was one of these men in his day; Lee Cranmer bade fair to carry on the work in worthy fashion—work taken up for a period by an Englishman named Wells, but abandoned for stories of a different and in my humble opinion, less absorbing—type.

Lee wrote three novels, all published which dealt with such subjects—two of the three secured from his own father's labors, and the other speculating upon the discovery and possible uses of inter-atomic energy. Upon John Corliss Cranmer's return from Prague that fatal winter, the father informed Lee that a greater subject than any with which the young man had dealt, now could be tapped.

Cranmer, senior, had devised a way in which the limiting factors in protozoic life and growth, could be nullified; in time, and with cooperation of biologists who specialized upon *karyokinesis* and embryology of higher forms, he hoped—to put the theory in pragmatic terms—to be able to grow swine the size of elephants, quail or woodcock with breasts from which a hundredweight of white meat could be cut away, and steers whose dehorned heads might butt at the third story of a skyscraper!

Such result would revolutionize the methods of food supply, of course! It also would hold out hope for all undersized specimens of humanity—provided only that if factors inhibiting growth could be deleted, some method of stopping giant-hood also could be developed.

Cranmer the elder, through use of an undescribed (in the notebook) growth medium of which one constituent was *agar-agar,* and the use of radium emanations, had succeeded in bringing about apparently unrestricted growth in the paramoecium protozoan, certain of the vegetable growths (among which were bacteria), and in the amorphous cell of protoplasm known as the amoeba—the last a single cell containing only neucleolus, neucleus, and a space known as the contractile vacuole which somehow aided in throwing off particles impossible to assimilate directly. This point may be remembered in respect to the piles of lumber left near the outside walls surrounding Dead House!

When Lee Cranmer and his wife came south to visit, John Corliss Cranmer showed his son an amoeba—normally an organism visible under low-power microscope—which he had absolved from natural growth inhibitions. This amoeba, a rubbery, amorphous mass of protoplasm, was of the size then of a large beef liver. It could have been held in two cupped hands, placed side by side.

"How large could it grow?" asked Lee, wide-eyed and interested.

"So far as I know," answered the father, "there is *no* limit now! It might, if it got food enough, grow to be as big as the Masonic Temple!

"But take it out and kill it. Destroy the organism utterly—burning the fragments else there is no telling what might happen. The amoeba, as I have explained, reproduces by simple division. Any fragment remaining might be dangerous."

Lee took the rubbery, translucent giant cell—but he did not obey orders. Instead of destroying it as his father had directed, Lee thought out a plan. Suppose he should grow this organism to tremendous size? Suppose, when the tale of his father's accomplishment were spread, an amoeba of many tons weight could be shown in evidence? Lee, of somewhat sensational cast of mind, determined instantly to keep secret the fact that he was not destroying the organism, but encouraging its further growth. Thought of possible peril never crossed his mind.

He arranged to have the thing fed—allowing for normal increase of size in an abnormal thing. It fooled him only in growing much more rapidly. When he came back from Cuba the amoeba practically filled the whole of the mud sink hollow. He had to give it much greater supplies. . . .

The giant cell came to absorb as much as two hogs in a single day. During daylight, while hunger still was appeased, it never emerged, however. That remained for the time that it could secure no more food near at hand to satisfy its ravenous and increasing appetite.

Only instinct for the sensational kept Lee from telling Peggy, his wife, all about the matter. Lee hoped to spring a *coup* which would immortalize his father, and surprise his wife terrifically. Therefore, he kept his own counsel—and made bargains with the Cajun, Rori, who supplied food daily for the shapeless monster of the pool.

The tragedy itself came suddenly and unexpectedly. Peggy, feeding the two Gordon setters that Lee and she used for quail hunting, was in the lodge yard before sunset. She romped alone, as Lee himself was dressing.

Of a sudden her screams cut the still air! Without her knowledge, ten-foot *pseudopods*—those flowing tentacles of protoplasm sent forth by the sinister occupant of the pool—slid out and around her putteed ankles.

For a moment she did not understand. Then, at first suspicion of the horrid truth, her cries rent the air. Lee, at that time struggling to lace a pair of high shoes, straightened, paled and grabbed a revolver as he dashed out.

In another room a scientist, absorbed in his notetaking, glanced up, frowned, and then—recognizing the voice, shed his white gown and came out. He was too late to do aught but gasp with horror.

In the yard Peggy was half engulfed in a squamous, rubbery something which at first glance he could not analyze.

Lee, his boy, was fighting with the sticky folds, and slowly, surely, losing his own grip upon the earth!

IX

John Corliss Cranmer was by no means a coward. He stared, cried aloud, then ran indoors, seizing the first two weapons which came to hand—a shotgun and hunting knife which lay in sheath in a cartridge belt across hook of the hall-tree. The knife was ten inches in length and razor keen.

Cranmer rushed out again. He saw an indecent fluid something—which as yet he had not had time to classify—lumping itself into a six-foot-high center before his very eyes! It looked like one of the microorganisms he had studied! One grown to frightful dimensions. An amoeba!

There, some minutes suffocated in the rubbery folds—yet still apparent beneath the glistening ooze of this monster—were two bodies.

They were dead. He knew it. Nevertheless he attacked the flowing, senseless monster with his knife. Shot would do no good. And he found that even the deep, terrific slashes made by his knife closed together in a moment and healed. The monster was invulnerable to ordinary attack!

A pair of *pseudopods* sought out his ankles, attempting to bring him low. Both of these he severed—and escaped. Why did he try? He did not know. The two whom he had sought to rescue were dead, buried under folds of this horrid thing he knew to be his own discovery and fabrication.

Then it was that revulsion and insanity came upon him.

There ended the story of John Corliss Cranmer, save for one hastily scribbled paragraph—evidently written at the time Rori had seen him atop the wall.

May we not supply with assurance the intervening steps?

Cranmer was known to have purchased a whole pen of hogs a day or two following the tragedy. These animals never were seen again. During the time the wall was being constructed is it not reasonable to assume that he fed the giant organism within—to keep it quiet? His scientist brain must have visualized clearly the havoc and horror which could be wrought by the loathsome thing if it ever were driven by hunger to flow away from the Lodge and prey upon the countryside!

With the wall once in place, he evidently figured that starvation or some other means which he could supply would kill the thing. One of the means had been made by setting fire to several piles of the disgorged timbers; probably this had no effect whatever.

The amoeba was to accomplish still more destruction. In the throes of hunger it threw its gigantic, formless strength against the house wall *from the inside;* then every edible morsel within was assimilated, the logs, rafters and other fragments being worked out through the contractile *vacuole.*

During some of its last struggles, undoubtedly, the side wall of brick was weakened—not to collapse, however, until the giant amoeba no longer could take advantage of the breach.

In final death lassitude, the amoeba stretched itself out in thin layer over the ground. There it succumbed, though there is no means of estimating how long a time intervened.

The last paragraph in Cranmer's notebook, scrawled so badly that it is possible some words I have not deciphered correctly, read as follows:

> "In my work I have found the means of creating a monster. The unnatural thing, in turn, has destroyed my work and those whom I held dear. It is in vain that I assure myself of innocence of spirit. Mine is the crime of presumption. Now, as expiation—worthless though that may be—I give myself . . ."

It is better not to think of that last leap, and the struggle of an insane man in the grip of the dying monster.

• • • • •

About the Author

Anthony M. Rud. Portrait by Hubert Rogers

Anthony M(elville) Rud was born in Chicago, Illinois, on January 11, 1893, to Dr. Anthony and Dr. Alice Rud. In 1914, Rud graduated from Dartmouth College and went to study medicine at Rush Medical College. Soon he discovered the medical profession was not for him.

By 1918, Rud turned his attention to writing fiction and met with success selling to *Green Book Magazine.* Over the next four years he would place manuscripts with *Top Notch, Argosy, Saturday Evening Post, Popular Magazine, Smith's Magazine, People's, Sea Stories, Action Stories, Black Mask* and *Short Stories.* Several novels were soon to follow.

In 1923, Rud left Chicago to accept an associate editorial position with Doubleday, Page Co. in New York, publishers of *Short Stories, Frontier* and later *West* magazines. Four years later he took over the editorship of *Adventure.* But his heart was in creating his own fiction. He resigned this position after two years to devote himself to freelance writing.

Over the next twelve years, Rud turned out a steady production of adventure and mystery stories for the better paying pulp markets such as *Argosy* and *Blue Book* and created the Jigger Masters series for *Detective Fiction Weekly.*

His life was cut short when he suffered a fatal heart attack on November 30, 1942, at age 49.   TOM ROBERTS

Novelty—The Essential of Science Fiction

CHARLES D. HORNIG

Mr. Hornig, managing editor of Wonder Stories, *is the youngest holder of this title in the national field, being only seventeen years of age. For his own amusement and in the advancement of weird fiction, he launched The Fantasy Fan in 1933 and still edits it. When this little experimental magazine came to the attention of Hugo Gernsback, it led to the appointment of Mr. Hornig as managing editor of* Wonder Stories.

The dictionary defines evolution as the "act of development." Scientists have proved that every living thing in the world undergoes evolutionary changes. We cannot perceive these changes in nature because of their infinite slowness. Nature does not work fast—but man sometimes does. Nature has all eternity in which to accomplish her tasks—but man must progress all he can during his brief lifetime, which is but the wink of an eye in comparison to the Greater Forces. His mechanical inventions best illustrate this point. Most or us have been astounded by the rapid strides taken in the fields of aeronautics, automotives, radio, and other lines of research.

In the writing field, evolution is due chiefly to the ever-changing tastes of readers. They tire after awhile of any particular brand of story, and even though it may have caused quite a sensation when it first appeared, the style will eventually become boring. The phrase, "Familiarity breeds contempt," can be applied to fiction. Even too many luxuries—too many of anything—will, become boring and uninteresting after a time.

Science fiction has the peculiarity of being the fastest-changing fiction in existence. It is also the youngest on the market. Even ten years ago, it was little known.

In the early days of science fiction, I should say before 1930 (for before then it did not undergo noticeable changes), there was no such thing as a hackneyed plot; there had not been enough stories written around one theme to make it become hackneyed! The ideal story of those days was the one in which our brave earth-man built himself a space-ship, went to Mars, conquered the enemies of the most civilized of the Martians (who were invariably human beings), which he usually did single-handed, and then married the princess with whom he had fallen in love. The Martians had probably mastered telepathy and used death, disintegra-

Reprinted from *Author & Journalist,* July 1934.

tion, and paralyzing rays. The primary requisite of the tale was to be fantastic, and the science was only secondary.

Another one of these old plots was that in which a mad scientist attempted to conquer or destroy the earth, but whose plans were thwarted at the last minute by some young fellow not more than twenty-five. And then we had the wonderful inventions that exploded just before they were about to be given to the suffering world.

On the other hand, we had science fiction with the science accented and the story almost non-existent. It was usually an elaborate description that the scientist gave to his assistant, of some discovery or invention. It contained practically no plot. And there was the story that served principally as a vehicle for describing the author's conception of an improved social system.

Of course there were some classics in the old days that do not come under these categories, such as Merritt's *Moon Pool* and Serviss's *Second Deluge*, but the type of story I refer to is that which appeared most frequently in the science fiction magazines.

In the last few years, science fiction has undergone several definite changes. Most of the stories that were published five, six, and seven years ago would not be acceptable today. The evolution of science fiction can be likened to the motions of a pendulum—swinging from the purely fantastic to the purely scientific. Through the years, this swinging has slowed down, until the pendulum will soon be motionless—hanging at a happy medium between the two.

But an equal balance between science and fantasy is not the only requisite of the modern story; it must be logical and plausible in both its action and science. It is difficult to write, and a success in this field is truly a classic. The new science fiction should be so realistic that the reader lives with the characters and is absorbed to the point of distraction. He must be oblivious of all but the story. If he keeps turning the pages that are yet unread to see how much is left, the story is a failure. If he is reluctant to read "The End" on the last page, the story is a success. When a tale of this type is filled with love interest, it may show that the author has not faith enough in the science quality of the story to hold the reader's interest. This cannot be called true science fiction. The only readers who will enjoy the tale are those who also like the pure love story. This does not mean that there may be no love interest in the story—but it should not be dominant.

Some authors have the misconception that they can take a story that belongs in a Western or detective-story magazine, set it in the future, add a few rays and space-ships, change the locale from Texas or the East Side to Mars, and call it science fiction. The "scientale" is in a classification of its own. It uses the *improbable* but conceivably possible to produce sensations of amazement, wonder, and astonishment. You will notice that the science fiction magazines are named after these sensations.

The science story is a thing in itself, and the less it resembles the ordinary variety of story the better. This does not mean that there should not be an occasional bit of humor in these tales, particularly ironic humor, such as the type used by Stanton A. Coblentz, which shows up the mental and spiritual weaknesses of the human race in comparison with men of the future or of other worlds. Humor creates a pleasing effect in any story when properly used. David H. Keller has mastered it, and other authors have had occasional spurts of genius in this connection.

A story using an old theme or plot, though good when it first appeared, cannot produce any new sensation of awe or wonder in the reader, for he has already heard of such things before. Therefore it fails to achieve its desired effect. Originality, then, is the aim to be sought above all else. Most readers are tired of reading about ray wars, world-saving, mad scientists, dimensional terrors, and like subjects, and are demanding *new* ideas.

Some readers undoubtedly do not grasp what I mean, by *new*, and will think that my statements are too vague. This is only natural, for they are the ones that have never written a *new* story! If they had, they would know what I mean, for they would have experienced it. Their plots must be based on something that has never been used before in a story, preferably a plausible scientific theory that attempts to explain some mystery that scientists cannot solve at the present time.

The only way that I can clearly elucidate my point is to give some examples of the new ideas underlying stories that I have accepted for *Wonder Stories* recently.

"Evolution Satellite," by J. Harvey Haggard. Evolution is caused by an emanation from the core of the satellite Number One of Uranus. These invisible waves penetrate throughout the solar system, and the distance of each planet from the satellite determines the rate of evolution upon that particular world, so that Mars, being closer to the moon than Earth, would undergo a speedier change in its animal world. Life directly on the satellite evolves so fast that each creature goes through an entire cycle of evolution during its lifetime, and can adapt itself to its environment at a second's notice, no matter how often the environment changes or how radical are the differences. Therefore a plant that had never known fire would burn freely for a second and then prove forever invulnerable to it.

"The Sublime Vigil," by Chester D. Cuthbert. As scientists declare, the ether is everywhere—even in the vacuum of space. It is not a gas, liquid, solid, or vibration, but of a composition entirely different from anything else. This continuum is only distorted in the center of the greatest suns of the universe. In these suns, a "hole" is created in the ether, caused by the tremendous forces in the stars' centers. These "holes" travel away from the suns where they were created, along with the ether surrounding them, and usually repulse matter of any description. However, when they do touch a small tangible body, the body is absorbed into the "hole" to travel away into space with it. As nothing can exist where there is no ether, a body in one of these "holes" cannot change in the least. If it be living, it cannot die—it cannot live—it cannot grow old. If it is cast out a billion years later upon contact with another world, the creature that had been within the hole would not have experienced the lapse of even a second of time.

"Today's Yesterday," by Rice Ray (Russell Blaiklock). We are traveling along in time as if on the waves of an ocean. At the peak of each wave is a world. This series of waves, traveling through time, carries the worlds along in a chain of dimensions. While our world is passing through "today," the world behind us is passing through "yesterday." Therefore, could we travel to that world, we would be back in yesterday, though we would not be on the earth. Similarly, the world ahead of us, on the next wave crest, is traveling through "tomorrow," although it is "today" to the creatures on that world. Between the crests is a great divide that keeps the worlds apart, so that the first law of physics, "No two things can occupy the same space at the same time," can ring true.

"The Spore Doom," by Eando Binder. In this story, a fungus plant is developed by chemists during a war. When the spores are distributed through the atmosphere over the enemy's land, the plants spring up and destroy the crops. This nearly causes a famine. Then, as the author says, it starts a campaign of its own. It proves to be a blender of species, so that edible crops blend with poisonous plants, making a careful analysis necessary before anything grown can be eaten. After a few years, the freak fungus develops a plant that absorbs oxygen directly from the air in such huge quantities that the atmosphere of the earth becomes unbreathable. Man must burrow into the ground to live in air-tight cities and manufacture his own atmosphere. After a while, the blender of species is used by the scientists to develop a new plant that crowds out the oxygen-consuming one, making the surface of the earth once more habitable.

"The Spore Doom" by Eando Binder
Wonder Stories, February 1934

"The Man from Beyond," by John Beynon Harris. While this story does not introduce any new scientific theory, as do the ones preceding, it presents a new plot which makes it different from all others. An earth-man goes to Venus to find the planet in a prehistoric age. He enters a valley and becomes petrified, put into a state of suspended animation by certain gases emitting from a fissure in the ground. Everything else in the valley is petrified—animals and plants alike. Ages pass—untold centuries during which intelligent life evolves on the planet. During an expedition of the Venusians, the earth-man is brought from the valley and revived to life. He is put in a cage in the Venusian zoo for the gaze of the curious creatures of that planet, which are far from human in appearance. After several attempts, he convinces them that he is intelligent, and in the end is astounded to find out that humanity had vanished from the face of the

"The Man from Beyond"
by John Beynon Harris
Wonder Stories, February 1934

earth untold years before. He was the last of his kind in existence, kept alive by the forces of a younger planet.

These ideas, as far as I know, are altogether new—you have probably never heard of any just like them before. Each one is different from all others and therefore thoroughly absorbing to a science fiction fan.

An author can write *new* stories only by exerting his mental powers to the utmost. He will find it easier to write a story of scientific fiction if he first plans it out in detail, making sure that the central idea has not been used before, at least to his knowledge, before he sits down to type it out. If he knows beforehand what he is going to write about, he can build around it—just as it is easier to build a house with the architect's plans than to construct it blindly without any thought as to how it will look when it is finished.

Arthur J. Burks is one of those born authors who can sit down at the typewriter and begin typing a story without the slightest idea of how it will end, and the result is almost certain to be unique and original. However, there are relatively few authors of this kind.

I hope that science fiction authors who may chance to read this will keep in mind this essential thought of newness—novelty. It will greatly improve their chances of selling.

Science fiction is the most important literature
in the history of the world, because it's the history of ideas,
the history of our civilization birthing itself. . . . Science fiction
is central to everything we've ever done, and people who
make fun of science fiction writers don't know
what they're talking about.

—Ray Bradbury

WANTED:
Original Art

**Private collector
seeks to buy original art, both color
cover and black and white interior
illustrations. Interested in adventure,
science fiction, pin-up, Spicy
and many other genres.**

DOUG ELLIS
**13 Spring Lane
Barrington Hills, IL 60010
(847) 217-4241
pulpvault@msn.com**

*Artists interested
in include:*

Walter M. BAUMHOFER

Rudolph BELARSKI

Earle BERGEY

Frederick BLAKESLEE

Hannes BOK

Enoch BOLLES

Margaret BRUNDAGE

Ed EMSHWILLER

Edd CARTIER

Virgil FINLAY

Kelly FREAS

J.R. FLANAGAN

R.G. HARRIS

Roy KRENKEL

Tom LOVELL

H.W. McCAULEY

P.J. MONIHAN

Frank R. PAUL

Howard PARKHURST

Hubert ROGERS

George ROZEN

Jerome ROZEN

Norman SAUNDERS

Modest STEIN

J. Allen ST. JOHN

H.J. WARD

and many others!

107

The Science Fiction Field

LEIGH BRACKETT

I am sitting here staring my typewriter in the face, trying to think how to begin this article. There's so much to be said about science fiction. It's admittedly the screwball of the magazine family. It is also, regrettably, more or less a stepchild, inclined to be overlooked and even sneered at. Anyone who has taken the trouble to read a good science fiction yarn, and read it honestly, knows that the field is no more worthy of contempt than the detective, adventure, western, or any other—in fact, less, since pseudo-science books lure some very bright brains indeed, and names with strings of degrees flying after like tails on so many kites.

I don't know of any field of writing that offers more opportunity to the beginning writer; to the established man who wants a change; to any writer at all who has an imagination, a little tolerance, and the desire to have fun while he works. The rate of pay compares favorably with that in any other pulp group, and there is literally no limit to the adventures you can have. If you're tired of this planet, or system, or galaxy, throw it away and build a new one. You're God, with all creation to play around in.

They say you have to be a little crazy to write stf.* Well, maybe. But we don't think we're nuts. We think we're imaginative, and forward-looking, and even sometimes a little prophetic. Were we astonished at the War Department releases concerning the rocket gun, the jet-propelled plane, radar, and some other things they'll only hint at darkly? We were not. We've lived around those gadgets since we cut our teeth.

Take a look at the plans for the house of the postwar future. Take a look at television, plastics, new surgery, new techniques in psychological living. All of them have been forecast, used, and reused in the pages of the stf magazines. The brass hats already are swiping our terminology!

Maybe you're one of those people who will say, "Oh, sure, they make a few good guesses and all that, but it's still kid stuff. Nothing but a bunch of funny-looking monsters chasing around, or a Rube Goldberg machine that integrates fraldemors out of the palefranesus. Who wants that junk? An adult mind has to have something real to work on."

All right. Have you read the stories of Heinlein, De Camp, Hubbard, Leiber? The social histories of the future as they might well be written, with not one monster included. Have you read the exquisite other-world adventures of C.L. Moore,

* Stf, in the jargon of an ardent fandom, is a contraction of scientifiction and will be used therefore, if you don't mind, because stf is easier to type.

Reprinted from *Writer's Digest,* July 1944.

Kuttner's psychological masterpieces, the emotional "contemporary" yarn like Bradbury's "King of the Grey Spaces"? All of them as intelligent, as finely written, as searching, and a darn sight more thought-provoking than most of what you read in the top slicks.

Some of the greatest writers haven't been above writing stf. H.G. Wells, Conan Doyle, even Prime Minister Winston Churchill—so you needn't feel too snooty about it. The only measure of a man's pride in his work is the excellence of it, and the only time anyone needs to be ashamed of writing science fiction is when he writes it badly.

H.G. Wells

I'm not saying that there isn't childish stuff written and published. There is in every field of writing you can name. But too many people judge us all by the poorer comic strips.

Why should we be apologetic when we say we write for the fantasy field? We have Williamson. We have Hamilton. We have Wellman. We had Abraham Merritt, rest his soul. Why should we apologize? God knows there are enough novels perpetrated by Grade B morons.

I will say, however, that there seems to be a special type of psychology that goes with writing stf. Not everybody can do it, which is why the field is such a wide-open market for new talent. I can cite my own case, and in talking with other writers I have discovered that it has been more or less the same with all of them.

Childhood, by and large, is a long, dull period of supervision, orders, taboos, and general pushing-around by a variety of persons vested with authority and the power to enforce same. The inevitable result is that the child escapes mentally into a dream world where he is king and things are done to his liking. He is Robin Hood, he is Blackbeard, he is Tarzan. Some of these children, like myself, discover the most thrilling, the most tantalizing and fascinating realm of all—the kingdom of the imagination.

We enjoy riding the plains with Zane Grey, but we would rather walk the dead sea-bottoms of Mars under the little racing moons. We have found forests deeper and wilder than Sherwood, with giant trees lifting to a strange sun. We have furrowed seas more mystic than the Spanish Main. We have ridden the beasts of nightmare and peered into the canyons of the Moon. We have bridled the hippogriff under Koshtra Belorn, and there is nowhere, nowhere we cannot go.

As we grow older, we learn to our delight that many of these adventures we have had are possible. Some day men *will* be landing on other worlds than this, and much of this world is still secret and hidden. Our concepts of space and time and mass and relativity tell us that so much is possible, so many weird and incredible things going on constantly all around us. We are fascinated now with our minds as well as with our hearts and emotions. And it does something for us.

We who live half our lives in other worlds are never upset by anything new. We've always known it was coming. Because we're used to thinking in terms of whole solar systems, even whole galaxies, the cautious proddings of the post-war planners toward global thinking seem rather silly. We're not too much impressed by anything, and we have reams of literature, based on actual scientific data, exploring, almost every social trend, so we can hazard a fairly good guess about where every shade of thought is going to end up if it gets a chance. I'll be willing to bet that not one reader or writer of stf was among those stampeded by the famous Orson Welles broadcast. We'd all have been stampeding in the other direction—to get first look at the Marshies and then pump each other's hands delightedly while yelling, "I told you so—there *is* life on Mars!"

The point I'm trying to make is this—unless you have always read and loved fantasy (using the term in its broad sense), the chances are you simply haven't any taste for it, and unless you have you had better give the field a wide bye. Perhaps in no other type of writing is it as important to believe implicitly in what you are doing. Detective stories, westerns, all other types of fiction use backgrounds readily recognizable to the reader. In stf you build your own background out of the raw stuff of your creative mind, and unless you are so sure of it that you could draw a map, sketch a brief history and outline the culture of the inhabitants, nobody else is going to be sure of it either. We like our worlds, and we get a kick out of doing this. If you don't, stf is not for you. And please, for God's sake, don't think you can write down to the market. Editors have enough trouble as it is.

Having led you subtly to it, I shall now spring my second conclusion. I shall even put it in italics because I believe it so thoroughly and because it gave me my start as a professional: *There is no field of writing so well adapted to the needs of the very young writer who has not yet seen much of this world.*

Beginners are forever being told to write about life in their own backyards. But most young people are bored as hell with life in their own back yards. They've lived too much of it themselves, and it's going to take time and perspective to get the taste out of their mouths. So they try writing about Buda Pesth and Paris and the Old Manor at Trembling-on-the-Brink, and collect endless rejection slips, and become very sad characters indeed.

The weakness in this system, of course, is that a lot of people have been to Buda Pesth and Paris and the Old Manor. They know how the people there act and talk, what the streets look like, and how the cooking smells at dusk. Furthermore, because the tyro doesn't know these things, the blood of life is not in his stories, and even people who haven't been farther away from home than the corner grocery know that they are hollow and without truth.

Suppose, then, that this restless young writer decides to set one of his yarns on Mars. No one has been to Mars, at least not lately. No one can rise and scream, "Kahora doesn't look like that!" or, "That's not the way the caravans go from Ved to the Wells of Tamboina!" All the kid needs to do is read a few non-technical books on what science knows or guesses about Mars, take what he wants, modify it to suit, and knock together his own personal Mars, on which he can do as he pleases and no kicks from anybody.

Furthermore, because there is such a wide latitude of characters to choose from, the young writer is less apt to betray a lack of knowledge about people. The more he has, of course, the better—and this is the writer's chief purpose in life, to learn about people. But he can afford to let his imagination run away with him in dealing with extraterrestrial beings, human, semi-human, and monstrous. He will find that he loves these imaginary creatures with a peculiar and passionate devotion, because they are his own fears and hopes and desires speaking out with the voice he himself has given them.

Let's say I want to write a story about India. The closest I ever came to India was Kipling and a lone Sikh with bow-legs I pass occasionally in Pershing Square. It's obvious that in trying to handle the character of, say, a Pathan warrior, or perhaps a Hindu prince, I would fall flat on my face. Four years ago, when I sold my first yarn to *Astounding Stories*, I was doing just that with characters a lot closer to home than India. But I could take my readers into the hollow heart of a dark planet between Mercury and the Sun and introduce them to a flaming Child born of the Sun itself, and make them believe it. I *understood* that creature. I didn't always, or even most of the time, understand the people I passed in the street, but I understood the Sun-Child because it was an expression of my own longing for freedom, for strength—the galaxy to play with, racing the comets out on the edges of creation, drunk with the sheer immensity of space. The fact that the Sun-Child was imprisoned in a dark shell was, I suppose, symbolic of my own frustration. But we freed it, the hero and I, and I suppose that, too, was a symbol. Anyway, I got personal pleasure out of the whole thing, as well as a very nice check.

In this sense, writers of stf have an advantage over craftsmen in other fields. Frequently sheer power of imagination translated into mood, atmosphere, and unusual, compelling extraterrestrials will carry a story otherwise undistinguished in plot and characterization.

Perhaps you like stf and want to write it, but are scared off by that word "science." You're no Ph.D., and aren't likely to be, and you are thrown into a panic of inferiority by casual references to discontinuous functions in a four-dimensional space-time grid. Well, brother, you would be surprised how many top-notch stf writers don't know any more about it than you do. That same terror of ignorance held me off, too, although I was crazy to write the stuff, until a certain young man who was already big-time material in the game confided in me that all the science he knew could be put into a quart bottle and still leave room for a fifth of Scotch. Then I began to perceive that there's a trick to it.

There are, to be sure, quite a few stf men who are brilliant scientific minds, including professors of physics, engineers, etc. Their stories are impressively larded with advanced math and all the other super-scientific gimmicks that leave us simple souls politely dazed and gaping. I often wish I were smart like that. But I'm not, and still I get by all right and have a lot of fun doing it.

John .W. Campbell, Jr.

There are few editors who insist on heavy science—John .W. Campbell, Jr., of *Astounding Stories* being the notable example. But even Mr. Campbell will buy stories completely lacking in this regard, so long as they are well done and unusual. Also, many of his important novels are based on the human sciences—psychology, sociology, etc.—which are comprehensible to any intelligent person who is interested in them. (The beauty of the human sciences is that they're inexact, abounding in conflicting theories, and it's fairly hard to get tripped up—whereas, as I know to my sorrow, blundering around with chemistry is an invitation to disaster.)

To be sure, you must have some grounding in science. Impress this firmly in your mind: *You cannot contravene a known and accepted principle of science unless you have a logical explanation based on other known and accepted principles.* You must take into account all the basic laws of gravity, magnetism, electricity, atomic structure, astronomy, velocity, and all the rest. This requires research, and there are many nontechnical books available. Inasmuch as you have to observe the same rules in any story—to avoid, for instance, glaring blunders in police procedure when doing detective stuff—this shouldn't cause any trouble. Also, it's interesting to know what goes on in the world about you.

There's a wide range of material in stf, from the frankly juvenile on up. And the readers, barring a few heavy-science fanatics, look for the same things you look for when you read—entertainment, release, an emotional punch, a stimulus to the imagination. If you can give them that, let the four-dimensional space-time grids go hang. Most of us fans skip that part anyhow, so we can get on with the story.

Let's take a look at the mechanics involved in putting stf on paper and collecting checks for same.

If you're an old fan, you're probably painfully aware of all the cliches. If not, I advise you to read all the stf mags you can get hold of and learn what is overdone. The mad-scientist plot is on its last legs, thank God. The dictator-who-wants-to-rule-or-destroy is getting frayed around the edges from over use. And

unless you have an especially fresh and brilliant idea for the threatened or accomplished destruction of Earth, let the poor old girl have a rest. Ed Hamilton has
kicked her around enough already.

Space pirates are old stuff, and there has to be something more than blazing
ray guns and thundering rockets to pull them through. And the readers are tired of
the yarn based on the superhero and the ravishing babe (who seldom has a valid
excuse for being there anyhow) who get themselves all tangled up with bug-eyed
monsters on some planet, asteroid, or moon. This is the story replete with such
dialogue as, "My God, look there!" and such description as, "His square jaw set
grimly as he aimed his proton gun squarely into the gaping jaws of the advancing
monster."

When I was trying to break into stf,
the criticism was frequently made that my
stories were just present-day plots jazzed
up with ray guns instead of automatics,
and rockets instead of planes. Your stf
plot has to be part and parcel of its time
and setting. It must be integrated so that
that particular episode could not have occurred under any other circumstances of
locale and social conditions. You see why
you have to build solid backgrounds.

Planet Stories, Summer 1941

For instance, my novel "Shadow
Over Mars," which will appear soon in
Startling Stories, is based on the struggle
between various groups for the domination of Mars. There are the Pan-Martians,
fiercely resistant to any infiltration of out-
landers. There is the Terran Exploitations
Company, ruthless and greedy, crushing
Martian and Terran settler alike. There
are the Unionists, men of both races who want to use the best of both planets
to bring life back to a dying world. And, inevitably, there are the little guys of
both races who just want to be let alone, to live their own lives with decency and
hope. This is a situation which has occurred in pioneer America and other places,
I know. But the Martians, and the obstacles faced by the characters, are peculiar
unto Mars and themselves, a valid part of their own matrix. Furthermore, the old
piratical corporations here could only hope to dominate a small part of a conti-
nent. Only in the future, with interplanetary commerce and colonization, could a
company possibly hope to control an entire world.

It helps a great deal if you get a broad mental picture of what the world of the
future is apt to be like, taking into consideration logical developments in television, transportation, and so on. Some writers even make detailed chronological
charts. Decide what your own personal planets are going to look like, and stick to

it. This saves inventing whole new sets of names, natives, and conditions with each story, You'll find in reading stf that authors use the same cities and localities over and over, developing various races with individual traits and customs. If you are a reader of Brackett, for instance (and if you are a devotee of the best in stf you must, of course, be a reader of Brackett*), you will find references to the Low-Canals, the Jekkara spaceport, the trade-city of Kahora, the tribes of Shun and Kesh. On Venus the trade-city is Vhia. The Nahali with their scarlet eyes dance in the hot rains of the Middle Swamps, and pale giants with White hair done in intricate braids fight and laugh and sail their ships, sheathed in pearl shell, across the tideless sea. Mercury is a savage place of heat and mountain peaks that stretch up to space beyond the thin air, and the men who come from the Terran colonies of the Twilight Belt are as huge and darkly cruel as their native cliffs. All this makes for coherence in your stories, gives your readers something familiar to hang to, and it's always nice to go back and meet old friends. Let's drop in to Madame Kan's on the Jekkara Low-Canal, and drink green *thil* in tall glasses, and watch the little dark women dance, with the tinkling bells in their ears. Ah me! Would that I could . . .

Mr. Mathieu tells me to let you in on my formula, if any. Well, I've been trying to hook into other people's formulas these many, many moons, and so far I haven't been able to find one. They just look at me vaguely and say, "Well, I think, of a situation or a character or a setting that interests me, and then I get a guy in an awful mess, and—well, it just sort of builds from there."

If you're a struggling newcomer, you've read all the books there are on the subject, and I'll bet you don't know much more than when you started. You read the directions intelligently and they go into your head, but they don't flow through your fingers to the typewriter keys. And until those cold mechanical arrangements of character, complication, obstacle, suspense, and so on are translated into warm and vital beings as unconsciously as you breathe, you have not mastered the "formula." I am sadly convinced the only way to bring about this miracle is to write endlessly—to read and study and soak yourself in the stuff of other people's talents, to be sure, but most of all, to write. And write. And write.

There is a thing known as "plot sense." It is, like all the other tools of this maddening trade, an intangible. It is something developed over a period of time, absorbed from motion pictures, books, stories. You're developing this when you feel satisfied with a certain story, or feel unsatisfied with another. Most people just leave it there, but because you're a writer you'll want to know *why* you are pleased or displeased. Plot sense is the nameless little geek that sits on your shoulder, peering, and tells you to develop character here, or emotional reaction there, or to speed up and boot the reader in the guts on page nine. It's the monitor that keeps you from getting lost in the maze of possible futures you conjure up with the first word of your story.

Some writers never seem to get a firm grip on plot. W.R. Burnett, for instance, whom I admire immensely and who can't be beat for character and dialogue, commits sins of plotting such as ruined *The Quick Brown Fox*. Burnett should worry,

---

* If you aren't, you can quit reading this article right now, so there!

of course, but if he had a solid sense of plot he would never have had his big fascinating menace killed off-stage by a minor character, thereby leaving the book to fall like a punctured tire. I point out Burnett because he's good enough to get by anyway, and so say that if you are a genius you, too, can do it

Basically, the stf plot is no different from any other plot. It has to have the same elements of character, suspense, action, etc. The only difference is that in non-stf yarns you are limited by conditions already imposed by nature, history, and politics. In stf you are limited only by the conditions you yourself create, taking care to remain logically true to them.

The human characters in stf have to be as carefully drawn as people in any other field. Let Buck Rogers and Superman remain king in their own domain, and concentrate on genuine three-dimensional men and women. People in the year 3044 will love and hate and laugh and cry just as they were doing in 1944. Women will have babies, men will die for their beliefs. Their clothes, food, and entertainment will be as familiar to them as ours to us. They'll squabble over politics, rob and kill each other, moan over the younger generation, and give up safe homes on Earth to go pioneering on the frontiers of alien planets, just as our ancestors went to Oregon and California.

The guy that boots his tin kettle around the Triangle trade-routes—Earth-Venus-Mars—won't be any more a superman than the transport pilot of today. There will be heroes and scoundrels, but they will be no less human than the Colin Kellys and the John Dillingers of our time. They will be motivated by the same psychology and emotional habit-pattern that motivates you, or the guy next door. The stimuli may be different, but that's all.

The human story is the backbone of stf, say what you will about ultra-scientific gimmicks. And the farther you can stay away from steely eyes, bulging biceps, snarling ray guns, and bug-eyed monsters, the better off you will be.

Most of my own heroes are fairly hard boys, not above using their boot-heels in a scrap and giving a handsome wench one of those 40-second Bogart-type kisses. They're not invincible. They can be downed when the opposition is too tough. They're a fairly seamy bunch, because to me people who have bucked the realities of pain and hunger and fear are a lot more vital, more natural, than people well insulated by money and the inhibitions of custom.

I use women when the story calls for it. A novelette usually does. If there's no logical reason for a woman, she stays out. And this, little kiddies, brings us to the delicate subject of Sex in science fiction. All those under 21 please turn to next page.

There is nothing wrong with sex, in stf or out of it. To be sure, much of the sex stuff, politely termed romantic interest, is the same puerile sugar-icing crap you get in all the magazines, from *Terrible Tales* up to *For Snobs Only*. The heroine is a vision of feminine loveliness. (She usually does nothing but have tantrums, shriek, and generally gum up the action so that any normal man would let her have a stiff one to the button, but let that go.) He and she exchange a little light banter, usually at its cutest just as destruction closes in on them. They wouldn't dream of making a pass at each other. In fact, it always takes them 6000 words to discover that they are, well, in love, and they're always just as astonished and flustered as though they'd never heard the word before.

Well, if you like that sort of thing, fine. But if you don't, I inform you happily that you can get away with practically anything as long as it's well and subtly done, and you don't try to emulate Hemingway and James Gain. This does not mean that you can become vulgar and offensive, and an affair based on sex alone, with no deeper emotional meaning, would be out of place as well as dull. But sensitive, adult writing can put over equally adult situations. If you don't believe me, take a look at C. L. Moore's last novel for *Astounding*.

From my own work ("Thralls of the Endless Night," *Planet Stories*, Fall, 1943) here is a case in point. The setting is a lost colony of Earthmen, wrecked long ago on an asteroid far from the Sun. Generations of environment have wrought changes in them, a degenerate evolution returning slowly to the primitive. A boy and a girl are trapped, alone in a bleak wilderness, facing death.

A strange cold terror took him. He turned his head toward the yellow girl and saw the same thing in her eyes. They looked at each other, not moving nor breathing, thinking that they were young and going to die.

He shivered. The girl's golden body burned in the grey light. He moved. He didn't know why, only that he had to. He took her in his arms and found her lips and kissed them, roughly, with an urgent, painful hunger. She fought him a little and then lay still against him.

If that ain't sex, brother, I don't know what is. It is also, I think in my humble way, truth. My women are usually on the bitchy side—warm-blooded, hot-tempered, but gutty and intelligent. I like them, and I have fun working with them. I find that a great deal can be accomplished, when the temperature gets too warm, by simply slapping the space lever twice and letting the reader fill in the gap himself. Just try to be honest,

"Thralls of the Endless Night," by Leigh Bracket
Planet Stories, Fall, 1943

not dirty, and you'll be okay.

Next comes the question of ideas. People are always asking me how I think up these things, and I always give them the old saw about lobster and ice cream. But seriously, happenings in the news can be translated into the future. Put Rickenbacker's raft, for instance, in a Venusian ocean and see what happens.

The stories of other writers, particularly the classics, are fertile sources, and that doesn't mean plagiarism. Nobody can copyright a mood or an emotion. The idea for one of my favorite yarns, "Veil of Astellar", which will appear soon in *Thrilling Wonder Stories,* came from Lord Dunsany's tale, "The Man with the Golden Ear-rings." Another of my favorites, "The Halfling" which came out in *Astonishing Stories,* was inspired in part by *The Maltese Falcon* and the circus-of-the-future background just naturally grew out of Ringling Bros.

The physical properties of the worlds you create often suggest plots. I used to get my hero crashed or abandoned on page one and let him stagger off into the caves of Mercury or some place to see what he could see. The result was that Julie (Julius Schwartz, my guardian angel, sometimes spelled agent) wrote plaintively to please quit sending him so many stories beginning with just one guy going somewhere. A story, he pointed out, should have characters, plural. So let that be a lesson to you, too. Nonetheless, I still get yens to explore my private planets. A recent sale to *Planet Stories* was the result of interest in the ancient cities long buried under the warm and hungry seas.

Monsters—that is to say, creatures non-human and evolved under different environmental conditions—are a necessary adjunct to stf, and not to be sneered at unless they are crudely done. I always try to give

Thrilling Wonder Stories, Spring 1944

my queeps and fraldemors at least a touch of beauty and sympathy. I believe in them. I know where they came from, and why, and how. I am not interested in dull masses of flesh equipped with an unlikely array of fangs, tentacles, claws, mandibles, and glaring eyeballs, usually four of them mounted on stalks. Some of these e-t's (extraterrestrials, to you) are merely projections of our own dogs and horses and wild life. Others are your most fragile, or fascinating, or terrifying characters.

Planet Stories, March 1951

Be careful of your names, when christening people and places beyond this earth. I got a lot of complaints at first because most of mine looked like Zqfxl, which is difficult to pronounce and therefore annoying to the reader.

Well, and there it is. The trailways of space are before you, to blaze as you will. The editors of the science fiction mags are a swell bunch—my special and personal thanks to Alden Norton, Malcolm Reiss, W. Scott Peacock, Leo Margulies, and Oscar Friend. All the books have felt the paper pinch badly. But on the other hand, much of their big-name, big-producer talent is in service, or busy in Washington, so the gates swing for new blood.

I'll be looking for you when I get back. Right now my little Fitts-Sothern is warming up in the launching rack, ready to blast off for Venus. There's a situation developing there, up in the high plateaus north of the Sea of Morning Opals. I've got to see what happens.

Science Fiction Markets

Astounding Science-Fiction (Street & Smith), 122 East 42nd Street, New York 17. John W. Campbell, Jr., Editor.

Stories of high quality for intelligent readers. The scientific facts upon which a story is based must be accurate. But from there on imagination has unlimited scope. The author sets up a postulate, against which his story is told and must be completely self-consistent so that it will be acceptable to the reader. Lengths may run from 2500 to 60,000 words for fiction. Articles in the rotogravure section are usually written to order, but are open to any qualified writer. Query the editor first on these. A penname is permissible. But the subject must be handled authoritatively. Payment is on acceptance, at rates beginning at a cent and a half per word. Monthly.

Blue Book, 230 Park Avenue, New York 17. Donald Kennicott, Editor.

This magazine uses all sorts of adventure stories which will interest men readers. High quality of writing is important. Many of the contributors also sell to the *Post* and similar slick markets. An occasional science fiction story fits in. It must, of course, be unusual and be well done. Otherwise, there are no restrictions. *Blue Book* lengths include short-shorts; short stories averaging 5000 words, novels of about 50,000 words. But there is no such thing as an exact word-length here. Give a story what it needs; no more and no less. Payment is on acceptance at good rates. These vary with the length, author, and value of material. Monthly.

Famous Fantastic Mysteries (Popular Pubns.), 205 East 42nd Street, New York 17. Alden H. Norton, Editorial Director; Mary Gnaedinger, Editor.

The long novel featured in this magazine may be new material, or it may be reprint from a book—but never anything which has appeared before in a magazine. The novel runs up to 85,000 words. The market is open for short stories in lengths up to 10,000 words. These may be science fiction, fantasy, or weird stories. Payment is on acceptance, at one cent a word and up. A little poetry is also bought, at 25 cents a line. This may be filler length, or up to a page. Quarterly.

Planet Stories (Fiction House), 670 Fifth Avenue, New York 19. W. Scott Peacock.

All stories must have a basis of reasonable science. They may revolve around future-science, interplanetary adventures, spaceships, etc. But nothing is wanted which is just pure fantasy. The market is open to all lengths: shorts of 5000 to 6000 words; novelettes of 10,000 to 12,000; novels of 18,000 to 20,000. Payment is on acceptance. It varies from one cent a word up to a cent and a half per word. Quarterly.

Startling Stories (Thrilling), 10 East 40th Street, New York 16. Leo Margulies.

The lead novel must have a distinctly pseudo-scientific fantasy background. Length, 40,000 words. Shorts must be of the same type, and should be not over 6000 words in length. Payment is at a one cent minimum; on acceptance. Quarterly.

Thrilling Wonder Stories (Thrilling), 10 East 40th Street, New York 16. Leo Margulies.

All stories for this magazine must have a pseudo-scientific background. Occasionally fantasy too. The lead novel runs 15,000 to 20,000 words. Novelettes are 8000 to 10,000; shorts not over 6000 words. A few scientific articles are used. These should be no longer than 3000 words. Payment is promptly on acceptance, at rates beginning at one cent a word. Quarterly.

Weird Tales, 9 Rockefeller Plaza, New York 20. Dorothy McIlwraith, Editor.

This magazine includes a wide variety of fiction—weird, bizarre, unnatural, occult, vampires, witches, werewolves, ghosts. Included are a few science fiction stories. Lengths run anywhere from 3000 up to 10,000 words. Payment is one cent a word minimum, now approximately on acceptance. Bimonthly.

Amazing Stories, 540 North Michigan Ave., Chicago, Ill. Ray Palmer, Ed.

Stories have a solid scientific basis. 1-1/4c word, and up to 3c. Length, 2000 to 60,000.

Fantastic Adventures, 540 North Michigan Ave.,Chicago, Ill. Ray Palmer, Ed.

Fiction based on pure fantasy. Rates, lengths same as above. Science stories of the future or of today carried to imaginative heights. Unrestricted themes.

Around the Globe Adventure
from Black Dog Books

THE ADVENTURES OF JEHANNUM SMITH
GORDON MacCREAGH

For the first time in book form are the short stories and novel-length escapades of a two-fisted adventurer in Southeast Asia. With an introduction by Tom Roberts.

THE SAMOVAR GIRL
FREDERICK F. MOORE

A soldier returns to post-Revolutionary Russia seeking to kill the man who murdered his father. But he does not factor in meeting a beautiful samovar girl ... Will she aid him or denounce him?

THE SAGA OF THADY SHEA
H. BEDFORD-JONES

A man stumbles into the middle of a fight for mining rights in the American Southwest.

BLACK DOG BOOKS
1115 Pine Meadows Ct.
Normal, IL 61761-5432

www.blackdogbooks.net I info@blackdogbooks.net

Follow us!
Twitter.com/blackdogbooks1
Facebook.com/blackdogbooks1

E.E. "Doc" Smith Correspondence to Jack Darrow, 1931-38

DOUG ELLIS

Jack Darrow (a penname for Clifford Kornoelje) was a well known science fiction fan in the 1930s and early 1940s. He is mentioned often in Sam Moskowitz' history of fandom, *The Immortal Storm,* and for a time in the 1930s was right up there with Forrest J. Ackerman in terms of his prolific correspondence to the SF pulps. In fact, the meeting of Darrow and Ackerman at the first Worldcon in New York in 1939 was captured by several fan photographers, and billed as the meeting of SF fandom's top two fans. In addition to writing letters of comment on nearly every SF magazine published in the early and mid-1930s, Darrow also corresponded with many SF authors. Chief among these was his lifelong friend, Otto Binder (who with his brother Earl wrote as Eando Binder). Others included Jack Williamson and Edmond Hamilton, as well as one of early SF's greatest writers, E.E. "Doc" Smith. Darrow saved his correspondence with Smith and others, and after Darrow's death the material was sold at an estate sale in the Chicago area in June 2001. The following letters from "Doc" Smith to Darrow are an interesting look at the early days of the SF pulps, with a peek into his thoughts on several of his seminal series—including the info that he expected to end his classic Lensman series somewhat earlier than he actually did.

Edward E. "Doc" Smith.

Jack Darrow at the WorldCon 1,
New York City, 1939.

33 Rippon Ave.,
Hillsdale, Mich.,
April 21, 1931.

Mr. Jack Darrow,
4225 N. Spaulding Ave.,
Chicago, Ill.

Dear Mr. Darrow;-

Thanks immensely for your letter of yesterday.
Such letters as yours are particularly gratifying in that
I have read several of your letters to "Discussions" col-
umns in several magazines, and it has always seemed to me
that your remarks are well-balanced and carefully considered; rather the product of real thought and careful reading than the brainless and gushing outpourings so often
printed.

AMAZING STORIES has accepted a story I worked on
all last year, entitled "Spacehounds of the IPC". I do not
know when it is to appear, but they probably will announce
it shortly. It is the first of what may develop into a new
series---although of course it contains no bids for a sequel
in the shape of unfinished business, which I have always
regarded with hate and contempt---a series which I really
think will be more interesting and better in every way than
the "Skylark" series. You see, I thought that I had ended
that series definitely. I thought that everybody would
see that (probably with relief), and I did not expect to
hear a single demand for more. In fact, I have been constantly amazed at the reception given me, and the demand
for still another "Skylark". For a long time I refused to
write another---I could not really believe that there was
a real demand for one.

However, the publishers and I have both received
so many letters demanding a third "Skylark" that I started
to work on one some time ago. If I can do a good job on
it, it will probably be published by AMAZING STORIES late
in 1932---if not, it will be later than that, as I do not
want to spoil whatever good impression the "Skylarks" have
made by a cheap and hastily-written follow-up. And, as
you probably can understand readily, a third yarn in line
of progression with the first two is anything but easy
to write!

Regarding science in stories. Personally, I like
my scientific fiction really scientific. I like it wild
and fantastic, and the more highly improbable it is the
better I like it; but I do not like to read things which

are in direct contradiction to the every-day facts of
mathematics and observation---such as that awful thing in
a recent ASTOUNDING STORIES, which postulated a second
satellite of the Earth, behind the moon (and therefore
considerably farther away from the Earth than the moon)
and yet which HAD THE SAME PERIOD OF REVOLUTION AS DID
THE MOON). That kind of stuff gives me an acute and distinctly localized pain. Situations and episodes should
be remotely scientifically POSSIBLE; and I, personally,
like to have the details well enough explained so that I
can get a scientific picture of what the author is trying
to work out. It is much easier to write pseudo-science;
like ASTOUNDING STORIES wants---it is much easier to push
a button and fly off into space than it is to figure out
a remotely possible mechanism which will propel a car there.

However, I have been asked many times to write
a story of exactly that type, and for some time (in my
idler moments, when I did not feel like really serious
writing) I have been working on it. It will contain no
actual violations of elementary astronomy, physicsm or
arithmetic, so far as I am aware; but I am explaining
nothing scientifically. Drives, etc., have been known
so long to my characters that no explanation is either
necessary or desirable, and whenever any of my people
want to see around a corner or any other such trifle,
they have apparatus all ready to do it. I am putting
everything into it but the kitchen sink---everything in
my notes that was too wild to use in the "Skylarks" or
the "Spacehounds". It is only about half done, so I don't
know what I will do with it---it may be too wild even
for ASTOUNDING STORIES---but I must admit that I am getting
more fun out of writing it than I thought I would; and it
may be that you will see it in print some day.

I wonder how you will like it if you ever do
read it---"Doc" Smith writing pseudo-science?

Cordially yours,

Edward E. Smith,

Edward E. Smith, Ph.D.

33 Rippon Ave.,
Hillsdale, Mich.,
March 14, 1932.

Dear Jack:-

Thanks a lot for your letter of the sixth. I see that
your ideas haven't changed since our letters about a year ago.
But it is natural enough that you should prefer pseudo-science
to really scientific fiction. For the Skylark"---written in
1915-17---verged upon pseudo science; whereas "Spacehounds" was
really scientific fiction. I can readily understand that you
would like pseudo-science---I suggest only that you differentiate
better between scientific fiction and pseudo-science.

-       In this connection, I mentioned in my letter (did you
file it?) that I was writing a wild yarn of pseudo-science myself and was getting a big kick out of it. That story, "Triplanetary", is to appear in ASTOUNDING following Diffin's forthcoming
serial. I like it, myself, and think that you will, too---know-
ing from your published letters that that is one of your favorite
magazines. I like it, also. I think that it publishes the best-
written stories of any magazine of its type.

        I do not, however, care particularly for WONDER STORIES.
I read it, of course, and have a complete file of Gernsback's
magazines; but I do not see how I can write anything for it; at
least for some time. It wants pseudo-science, of about the same
type as ASTOUNDING, but does not pay high enough rates to secure
the best material; and, unlike the more prolific writers, I write
so slowly that I do not have to spread my stuff around to secure
an outlet for all I can write. I do not hurry, and I do not let
a story go until I think it is done. In fact, I have requests
from editors now for more work than I will be able to do for the
next two years---and since Gernsback does not seem to care particularly
whether or not I write for him, why should I bother?

        AMAZING has, of course, published a lot of filler; but
every once in a while they print a real gem, and they publish the
only real scientific fiction I know of. Hence my support---
AMAZING for its worth-waiting-for and priceless tales of really
scientific fiction; ASTOUNDING for its frankly pseudo-scientific,
but wonderfully well-written yarns.

        As you already know, I have been working for a long time
upon the third "Skylark", and it is now far enough along so that I
think I can do an acceptable job on it. Miss Bourne has been
asking about its progress for about two years, and I have just
given her formal notice that she could consider it in preparation.
But as to another "Spacehounds" I am doubtful. I have the data,
but, if written, they would have to appear in "Amazing Stories"
---ethics and type of story---and ASTOUNDING STORIES has already
asked me to begin another for them, even before "Triplanetary"
has appeared!

        So, how can I write for WONDER? However, if enough of
you WONDER fans write to Gernsback about me so that he will really
want a story of mine, he can probably get one.

                        Very cordially yours, Edward E. Smith, Ph.D

EDWARD E. SMITH. PH. D.
313 HOMECREST ROAD
JACKSON, MICHIGAN

May 8, 1938.

Dear Jack:-

     I have always said that I liked the boys best who wrote to
me the least---but you are really carrying matters to extremes.
For from 1932 to 1938 is six years: and, notoriously slow cor-
respondent that I am, I am quite sure that I could answer one
letter a year!

     Of course you're busy. So am I. So is everyone else
who hasn't given up---there simply isn't time enough on the
clock for anyone who is really alive. There is so much to do,
and so little time to do it in, that simply thinking about it
is enough to drive a guy nuts. Thus, I've got to work eight
hours a day to make a living for myself and the family; besides
the required outside reading and study, on things chemical.

     Then the reading I want to do---philosophy, physics,
astronomy; the science-fiction mags; fiction, biography. Then
there's an irreducible minimum of club and social activity---
the motorcycle club; about which my son and daughters howl bloody
murder if I miss too many events. Golf: if I don't get out there
often enough, my hook gets uncontrollable, my score gets up 'way
over 90 and I develop high blood pressure. Bowling ditto---my
average is something pitiful, and I used to roll in the 180's for
the season! Bridge---I have had to quit playing cards entirely.
I have a peach of a shop in my basement---carpenter, machinist,
radio---and that gathers dust most of the time. And I've simply
got to do some digging in the yard and some tinkering around the
house. And in my spare time I've got to write scientific fiction
stories---and now I am also working on a really serious novel---
about which it is too soon to say anything. TIME! Where does it
go to, and how? If I didn't have to work for a living at all,
and didn't have to sleep at all, I could still find useful and
highly enjoyable use for every minute of the 24-hour day!

     So you understand, I hope, why I let all the letters
pile up until I get ashamed of myself, and then answer them all
at once? But I usually do get them answered sometime; except in
some cases which I have allowed deliberately to lapse because of
lack of interest. You, however, would never be in that class.

     The ending of Galactic Patrol wasn't my fault---they
butchered it in the shop. I was in NY a couple of weeks ago and
went to the mat with them about it; but a correction now wouldn't
do any good---it's just so much soup under the bridge.

     I like Campbell, and think he's doing a swell job. In
fact, I like the whole Astounding outfit.

     Come again sometime, say about six months from now?

          Cordially,

Sink Your Teeth Into...

The Largest Inventory in the World!

Heartwood Auctions has more than 100,000 items in-stock! Our full-time team is hard at work getting these items onto our website, with weekly uploads for your browsing and buying pleasure!

With more than 25 years experience in comic art, vintage pulps, first editions, magazines, paperbacks and other collectibles, Heartwood Auctions has the experience and expertise to correctly grade and price every item, providing competitive rates and prompt, professional service.

So, whether you are buying or selling, one item or an entire collection - take a bite out of your collecting needs by visiting the Heartwood Auctions website:

www.heartwoodauctions.com

Heartwood Auctions
vintage pulps, magazines & books

—Buy & Sell—

WE BUY SINGLE ITEMS OR ENTIRE COLLECTIONS

Direct Purchase

Auction with Upfront Cash Guarantees

Consignment

NEW ITEMS POSTED FOR SALE EVERY FRIDAY!

Over 100,000 In-Stock!!

Most Accurate Grading in the Industry

Competitive Pricing

www.heartwoodauctions.com
954.565.8020 - sales@heartwoodauctions.com

Find us on Facebook

Henry Brandon as the irrepressible Fu Manchu and John Merton as his henchman, Loki, in *Drums of Fu Manchu* (1940).

Lobby card from *Drums of Fu Manchu* (1940).

From Pulp to the Silver Screen, 2013

Ed HULSE

This year we acknowledge the anniversaries of two very important events in the history of popular fiction. Ninety years ago the classic pulp magazine *Weird Tales* first appeared on the nation's newsstands, and one hundred years ago saw hardcover publication of Sax Rohmer's initial book featuring the insidious Dr. Fu Manchu. In celebration of these two milestones we present an assortment of feature films and TV episodes adapted from both sources.

Friday—

12:00PM
Drums of Fu Manchu (1940), Part One

The screenplay for Republic's 15-chapter serial did not adapt Sax Rohmer's book bearing the same title; instead it pilfered elements from the entire series, with a special emphasis on *Mask of Fu Manchu*. Reflecting the studio's large investment in character rights, *Drums* was more generously budgeted, and given a longer shooting schedule, than Republic's previous chapter plays. Added care was taken in scripting, casting, direction, and photography, resulting in what many believe to be the very best of the fabled Republic serials—an opinion shared, incidentally, by its co-director, William Witney. Henry Brandon is ideally cast as Rohmer's Devil Doctor and character actor William Royle, while not physically suited to the role of Nayland Smith, delivers what is certainly the finest performance of his mediocre career. We are proud to offer a unique presentation of this classic Fu film: a specially prepared feature version, broken into two parts, mastered by us from the only surviving 35mm print struck from the original camera negative. As the print was incomplete, our cut necessarily interpolates some footage from lesser-quality material, and the juxtaposition of sources will prove strikingly illustrative to those who've only seen inferior video editions released previously. Another Windy City exclusive!

2:00PM
Pigeons from Hell (1961)

In addition to the Fu Manchu centennial, this year's convention celebrates 90 years of *Weird Tales*, "the Unique Magazine," which retains its popularity among readers and collectors of classic pulp fiction. In its heyday *Weird Tales* failed to attract Hollywood film-makers, who presumably found most of its fare too outré for mainstream audiences. Only a couple yarns from the magazine made their way to the silver screen before 1960; we showed one of them, *Fiend Without a Face*, a few years back. *Weird Tales* was far better represented on the small screen, and this weekend we'll be revisiting some of the best TV versions of

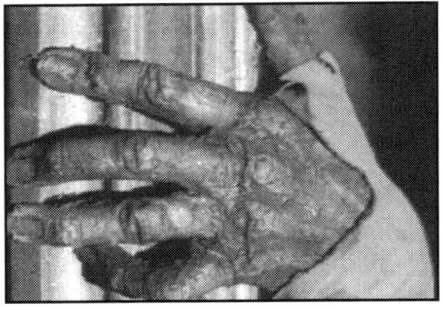

Pigeons From Hell (1961)

popular stories that debuted in the pulp. This 1961 *Thriller* episode marks Hollywood's first attempt at adapting Robert E. Howard. Originally published in the March 1938 issue of *Weird Tales* and called "one of the finest horror stories of the century" by Stephen King, *Pigeons from Hell* unfolds in and around an old mansion said to be cursed by a malevolent entity. Boris Karloff hosts the episode, which stars Brandon De Wilde and Crahan Denton.

3:00PM
Daughter of the Dragon (1931)

Having ignored his most famous character for more than a decade, Sax Rohmer was induced to revive the Devil Doctor at least partially in response to Paramount's widely successful 1929 talkies, *The Mysterious Dr. Fu Manchu* and *The Return of Dr. Fu Manchu*, starring a pre-Charlie Chan Warner Oland. By virtue of its previous contract with the author, Paramount retained right of first refusal to the novel that followed, *Daughter of Fu Manchu* (1930), and promptly optioned the property. However, writer-director Lloyd Corrigan and his fellow scenarists jettisoned Ro-

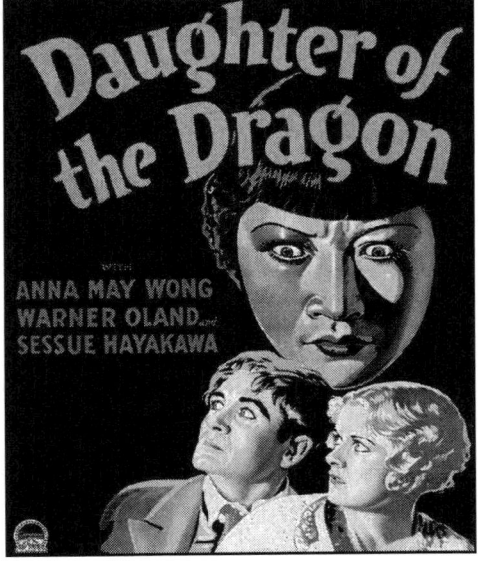

hmer's plot and substituted one furthering the revenge scheme that animated the previous two films. Fu's daughter, Fah Lo Suee, became Ling Moy, and the Doctor himself was killed off early in the proceedings. Nayland Smith was nowhere to be found, the cause of justice being represented by Chinese secret service agent Ah Kee. Rohmer purists are justified in denying *Daughter of the Dragon* admission to the canon, but the movie is quite engaging in its own right and certainly follows the melodramatic tradition of the author's best works. Moreover, it's a good showcase for early Hollywood's two prominent Asian-American stars: Anna May Wong and Sessue Hayakawa.

04:30
The Phantom Farmhouse (1971)

Back in the day, Seabury Quinn was the favorite author of many *Weird Tales* readers, and he was perhaps the most prolific as well. Strangely, his adventures of Jules de Grandin—some of which might have made dandy little "B" horror movies—were overlooked by Hollywood. The first of his yarns adapted to film was also his first published in *Weird Tales* (in the October 1923 issue, to be precise). *The Phantom Farmhouse* was broadcast early in the second season of *Night Gallery*, Universal's well-regarded series of supernatural stories. David McCallum plays the psychiatrist who comes under police questioning when one of his patients is found murdered under mysterious circumstances. Orson Welles, no stranger to dramas of this type, is the narrator.

David McCallum starring in *The Phantom Farmhouse* (1971)

Post-Auction:
The Mask of Fu Manchu (1932)

Most Rohmer fans believe this florid melodrama to be the best film featuring Fu Manchu. And it's hard to make a case to the contrary. The adaptation of the similarly titled novel (already written but not yet published when M-G-M purchased screen rights) hews fairly closely to the source, and the cast is nothing if not noteworthy. Grotesque makeup notwithstanding, Boris Karloff is superbly sinister as the Devil Doctor, Myrna Loy (then typecast as Oriental temptresses) suitably alluring as Fah Lo Suee, Lewis Stone stolidly dependable as Nayland Smith, and future cowboy star Charles Starrett properly heroic as

Boris Karloff in the lead role in *The Mask of Fu Manchu* (1932)

Terry Granville. For many decades after its theatrical release *Mask of Fu Manchu* was available only in a politically correct version that deleted numerous racially insensitive epithets uttered by the white cast members. Troublemakers that we are, our print restores the offending remarks in all their anti-Yellow Peril glory.

Saturday—

10:00
Drums of Fu Manchu, Part Two
The action moves to Asia as Fu Manchu races to beat Nayland Smith and his friends to the lost tomb of Genghis Khan. The second half of Republic's 1940 serial sacrifices some of the first half's spooky atmosphere but boasts a faster pace and outstanding action sequences, including some lifted from the studio's 1938 feature film *Storm Over Bengal.* For the record, our specially prepared cut eliminates repetitive situations from the serial's last third, which most fans agree was unnecessarily padded.

12:00
Yours Truly, Jack the Ripper (1961)
Few *Weird Tales* stories have been anthologized more than this Robert Bloch classic, first published in the Unique Magazine's July 1943 issue. *Thriller*'s

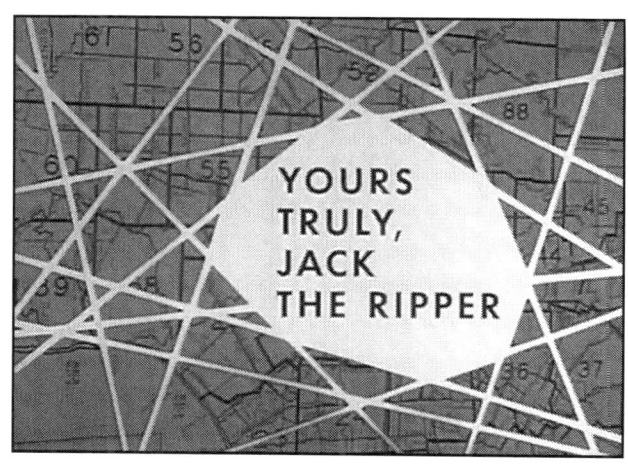

second-season adaptation boasts impeccable credentials: It was scripted by prestigious feature-film screenwriter Barré Lyndon, directed by well-regarded actor Ray Milland, and acted by an outstanding ensemble cast headed by John Williams and Donald Woods (with Boris Karloff on hand as host, of course). The story unfolds in New York, some 70 years after the original Ripper murders. A newly arrived British nobleman believes that Jack is still alive—eternally young as a result of some deal with the devil—and once again practicing his grisly craft in the Big Apple's sleaziest streets.

01:00
Masquerade (1961)

Henry Kuttner's blackly humorous short story from the May 1942 number of *Weird Tales* was the source for one of *Thriller*'s most memorable episodes. Years, in fact *decades* later, fans of the series could recall the twist ending even if they couldn't remember the story's title or plot details. Tom Poston and Elizabeth Montgomery play a young couple, lost while on their second honeymoon and presumably at the mercy of a family of cannibals running the ramshackle Southern hotel in which they've sought shelter. The couple, initially inclined to laugh off their spooky surroundings, accidentally uncover a shocking secret.

Elizabeth Montgomery and Tom Poston in the *Thriller* broadcast of "Masquerade."

02:00
The Face of Fu Manchu (1965)

The first of five Fu Manchu movies produced by Harry Alan Towers and starring Christopher Lee as the Devil Doctor. Towers, who scripted the film under his *nom de plume* of Peter Welbeck, didn't adapt a particular Rohmer novel but incorporated bits and pieces from several. *Face of Fu Manchu* takes place largely in London but was shot mostly in Dublin. As its melodramatic thrills were very much of a piece as those found in Edgar Wallace novels, Towers

The Face of Fu Manchu (1965) starring Christopher Lee.

cleverly cast German actors Joachim Fuchsberger and Karin Dor in key supporting roles; having co-starred in several of their country's wildly popular
Wallace adaptations, they lent considerable box-office allure to Towers' mod-
estly budgeted film, especially throughout Europe. Although the production
values are skimpy—with period detail particularly sloppy and inaccurate—
Face teems with action, suspense, and atmosphere. It's by far the best of the
Towers-produced quintet starring Lee as Fu Manchu.

03:45
The Whisperer in Darkness (2011)

Several years ago we ran *The Call of Cthulhu*, a privately produced, wholly faithful adaptation of H. P. Lovecraft's epochal *Weird Tales* story. Windy City attendees who praised that film will be delighted to see this sequel, also made under the auspices of The H. P. Lovecraft Historical Society. *Whisperer* actually expands on Lovecraft's original (first published in the August 1931 *Weird Tales*) while tale while still maintaining fidelity to it. Miskatonic University professor Albert Wilmarth tries to uncover evidence of strange creatures rumored to dwell in a mountainous region of Vermont. The investigation leads him to unimaginable horrors threaten his sanity as well as his life. Very stylish—and stylized—adaptation of a key Lovecraft tale.

Post-Auction:
Pickman's Model (1971)

Lovecraft's terrifying short story, first published in the October 1927 issue of *Weird Tales*, has been adapted by filmmakers five times to date, most recently last year. This version, which originally aired in 1971 as an episode of *Night Gallery*, was not only the first version but also the first Lovecraft yarn made for TV. Bradford Dillman, no stranger to troubled young men, plays eccentric art teacher Richard Upton Pickman, whose private studio becomes the scene of un-

remitting horror when a curious student follows him home. Not as faithful to the original story as subsequent adaptations, this version of *Pickman's Model* is not without merit and will make a satisfying cap to our weekend-long salute to *Weird Tales* on the small screen.

The Hugh Pendexter Library
from Black Dog Books

All editions authorized by the
Hugh Pendexter Literary Trust

ACCORDING TO THE EVIDENCE
HUGH PENDEXTER

Before Perry Mason there was The Bureau of Abnormal Litigation. Unravel the secrets behind these strange mysteries and happenings with investigative attorney Butterworth. First book publication. With an introduction by Jeremiah Healy, award-nominated author of the John Francis Cuddy mystery series.

"We know you will
enjoy [them] as much as we did."
—*Ellery Queen Mystery Magazine*

RED TRAILS

A Chronicle of Dunmore's War, pt.1
Life along the frontier was fraught with danger. With an introduction by Spur Award winning author and historian Troy D. Smith.

THE SHADOW OF THE TOMAHAWK

A Chronicle of Dunmore's War, pt.2
The US western expansion brings settlers into conflict with the Native Americans. With an introduction by Spur Award winning author and historian Troy D. Smith.

 BLACK DOG BOOKS
1115 Pine Meadows Ct.
Normal, IL 61761-5432

www.blackdogbooks.net I info@blackdogbooks.net

Follow us!
Twitter.com/blackdogbooks1
Facebook.com/blackdogbooks1

An Absorbing Mystery Story

"THE YELLOW CLAW"

beginning in Next Sunday's Feature Section of

The Plain Dealer

The latest work of that brilliant young author, Mr. Sax Rohmer.

Evening Telegram, (Elyria, Ohio) November 27, 1915

Index to advertisers

Adventure House (John Gunnison) 55, 83

Black Coat Press..13, 47

Black Dog Books (Tom Roberts) 17, 51, 121, 137

Ellis, Doug..107

Fantasy Illustrated (Dave Smith)..61

Heartwood Auctions 127

Mike Chomko Books 68

Pulp Radio (Roger Rittner Productions) 62

Schroeter, Rodney 62

Taraba Illustration Art 44

68063170R00077

Made in the USA
Middletown, DE
13 September 2019